EVERYTHING CHANGES: WHAT'S YOUR REAL SIGN?

Understanding Sidereal Time Zodiac

TRUDY PELLEGRINO

BALBOA.
PRESS

A DIVISION OF HAY HOUSE

Balboa Press books may be ordered through booksellers or by contacting:

Balboa Press
A Division of Hay House
1663 Liberty Drive
Bloomington, IN 47403
www.balboapress.com
1 (877) 407-4847

Print information available on the last page.

ISBN: 978-1-9822-3055-5 (sc)
ISBN: 978-1-9822-3054-8 (hc)
ISBN: 978-1-9822-3057-9 (e)

Library of Congress Control Number: 2019908802

Balboa Press rev. date: 06/29/2019

Forget Everything
You Know About Astrology
Until You Read This Book!

How does Sidereal Zodiac Affect You?
Find out if your sign changes!

True astrology is not locked in a
time frame of a seasonal calendar.
It is organically moving in space and time.

Table of Contents

Introduction

About the Author
and the Origins of this Book

I am a practicing Astrologer/spiritual advisor in a small metaphysical shop. Many people have walked thru the doors of this location and we have discussed much about astrology thru the years. I have noticed many people have a basic understanding of the twelve zodiac signs. They know which sign they are and talk about its attributes. Most people, though, have never gone much further in their exploration of astrology.

It is with much time and observation I will present the unique perspective on this other system of astrology. It has evolved for many years of speaking with my clients, hearing their reactions and applying the new sign to each and every one of them that my confidence in this system evolved. I invite you to forget everything you may have learned about astrology until you finish this book.

My inspiration to study of astrology started one Sunday morning in the 1987 while walking thru the Victory Gardens in Boston. A fellow on a bike with a straw basket tied on the front, one who your mom would tell you not to talk to, started up a conversation about astrology. He invited me to his friends Thursday night astrology study group. Though I never made it to the group, it did spark in me an interest in astrology.

This was back in book stores days, so I would search for information thru books and magazines available in the metaphysical section. The giant textbook available with the most complete information was Parkers Astrology. It became my go-to. I would use the ephemeris in the back of the book to see planetary locations, and with this book I learned to calculate charts by hand. I never trusted the accuracy of the charts, as I was an enthusiast, and at the time had no true teacher to confirm my homework. When computers became accessible and programs made chart calculations something I could trust, I compared my old charts to the computer and I had drawn accurate charts! Circa 2002 I started to sit down with clients with my new laptop and western astrology program.

Backing up a couple years, in 1996, my life had taken a turn, so I decided to have an astrology reading with an astrologer using Jyotish, the study of Astrology from India. The reading was surprisingly accurate with timing and events. I learned that he applied a different system of astrology. But he didn't explain anything about his astrology to me. Years later as I was reviewing my astrological software I saw that there indeed was another system of astrology other than the popular Tropical zodiac popular western astrology used. It was called Lahiri, or Sidereal time Zodiac. I never even thought once about changing systems, nor did I ever do much to learn what sidereal Zodiac or Lahiri even was.

In 2008 when I had opened the new shop location I needed to up my game with more astrology knowledge. Like most western astrologers, I was self taught and aligned with popular astrology. For decades I was happy in this Tropical zodiac. I was learning about the different ways Astrology worked and that was enough to keep me occupied. Slowly though I began to keep coming across the path of this different system, one that uses true star time. I'd check out this "Sidereal Time" option every now and then in the astrology program I had.

I remembered when I had that Jyotish Reading that I had a different chart and signs than western astrology. It set my chart up differently than western. What I eventually figured out was, it was aligned to Sidereal time. I had different signs. There was no book on a shelf to really explain this difference. So I had no formal reference, just these clues. Jyotish was aligned to Sidereal time. But what was Sidereal Time?

They say learning things thru experience is the only way to learn things! I finally discovered the truth in 2008. A friend was visiting and knew I was into astrology. He was showing off his new smart phone and a planetarium app that showed the planets in the sky. He held the phone towards the moon, and it revealed that the moon was in Taurus I was immediately confused. My computer program and popular astrology sites claimed the moon was in Gemini. Popular astrology did not correlate to what was actually in the sky. My world was shaken.

I had a clue that Sidereal time and Tropical time were different, but I finally saw how different. Jyotish, the ancient astrology of India, has always followed the stars in the sky. They use Spica as the fixed star to align their astrological data. As astrology has been accepted and held sacred in this spiritual cultural of India in temples by astrologers and priests, they have always been using correct and current astronomical data to chart their skies and apply it to astrology.

So surely you can understand, some turmoil started happening in my world. I was on my own to comprehend the difference, and it took a while to assimilate and to change systems. But once I did start experiencing Sidereal time and applying to myself and clients, I know this is the right fit.

I could feel astrology at work in a way I couldn't before.

It rings with the truth Astrology developed to hold. Then, finally, after being adrift in the self study of Astrology, I found an astrology teacher. Thru much yoga, kirtan, spiritual teachers and Gurus, I found a small astrology conference was happening thru an email. It was not far from where I live at Menla Mountain House, in Phoenicia, NY. I attended the conference which had western astrologers, a Tibetan astrologer and a jyotish astrologer. It was with the Jyotish teacher I went on to study many years with her in depth courses on the astrology from India, Jyotish.

Jyotish is a very vast, and fine tuned subject. In this book some information is a translation of my study of Jyotish, but we are not going into the complicated study of Jyotish. This is a simple book to clarify the two different systems, so that people may understand the less known Sidereal time better, and how they use astrology as well.

It can take time to understand the different systems, so take it easy. I have been introducing this system in my shop and observing peoples reactions for a decade. There are many people who get it right away, and others who may never understand the change. Only time and experience can make a true believer.

Here is some basic information as to what the two systems are, and you can better choose the system you use.

Chapter 1

The Two Systems

One Simple Fact

What Sign is the Sun in?

Tropical Zodiac
Origins of Tropical Zodiac

Sidereal Zodiac
What is sidereal time?

Whats Your Real Sign?

The Story of Sidereal Time Astrology

The Two Systems

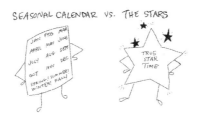

SEASONAL CALENDAR VS. THE STARS

There is something you might not know about astrology but assumed was true. Western astrology is not correlated to actual Astronomy. Most people assume that it is aligned accurately to whats currently in the sky. But actually it is adjusted back 24 degrees so that Aries can fit the first day of spring.

Many people are floating with limited information on the surface of pop culture astrology. Yes, it is a fun game to learn and play, and most people can tell you their sun sign thru having applied their birthdate in a tropical zodiac astrological calendar. But there is a sacred side of astrology that brings much truth. It works if you tune in.

Pulling a couple of tarot cards, people can get a reading. So even if your astrology is not correctly aligned, you going to get a reading. The reader can intuit some things. But if you get it correctly aligned, Astrology is really magical and can give you a very accurate reading!

Thru my observation at the shop I found two areas that go hand in hand that I think need clarifying.

1. On a spiritual level, popular astrology may be the most limiting system you could use. To sum yourself up as a "sign" is the furthest

thing from spiritual you could do. It is more ego defining and clinging to some limited view of ourselves. You are way more than just your sign. It is best to consider the entire chart or sky at the time of your birth. The 'birth chart' is a divine pattern of light and energy that reveals an essence of who you are. Considering the birth chart brings self understanding, growth and removes our own self created obstacles. Everyday brings new planetary and universal energies. It is impossible to ever be just "a sign."

2. On a technical level, I needed to explain this exciting discovery i made about astrological systems that most people involved in popular astrology almost never find out. Popular modern day astrology, applies Tropical Zodiac, a system that aligns it self with Seasons, based on the way the Sun influences the earth. This system isn't following true astronomy.

It does apply astronomy, accurate information about the planets and their movement, but then it is shifted back 24 degrees to the first day of spring and call it Aries. The astronomical first day of Aries is currently April 14. The first day of spring the sun is actually in Pisces at 6 degrees. When we re-align astrology to astronomy, it puts many people with a different Sun sign then what they thought they had using the Tropical popular culture system.

This gap is called the Ayanamsha and is a legitimately recognized issue, mostly by Eastern astrologers who recognize the Western astrologers dont know what they are doing with tropical zodiac. There is more about this in upcoming chapters.

Of course any good scientific exploration needs a little time in the lab to test out the theory to make sure it works. In the shop I made a chart of Sidereal time Zodiac set out for all to see, mostly as a teaching tool about the system. People were curious and asked often about this different system. The more people that offered their birthdate and applied it to the sign, the more I was gaining insight and assessed their sign to this system of astrology. It was easy to see how this system was aligning in the truth. In fact, many revealed how they never even felt like their sign in Tropical zodiac. The upcoming chapters will help to explain the details of this discovery.

To get your first glance of your new sign, check out the chart below. This is a replica of the chart I have used in the shop as a teaching tool. Find out your new sign and understand better this "new" system of Astrology.

Each sign is 30 degrees.
The sun travels one degree per day.
Since 24 degrees is the gap between systems
it puts 24 days having a different sign,
While 6 remain in an overlap.

True Sidereal Time Zodiac

ARIES- April 14 to May 14
TAURUS- May 15 to June 14
GEMINI- June 15 to July 16
CANCER- July 17 to August 16
LEO- August 17 to September 16
VIRGO- September 17 to October 16
LIBRA- October 17 to November 15
SCORPIO- November 16 to December 15
SAGITTARIUS- December 16 to January 14
CAPRICORN- January 15 to February 13
AQUARIUS- February 14 to March 14
PISCES- March 15 to April 13

You might have seen or heard about some news article about a new sign, or different alignment. Lately there has been a spin about the popular "13th" sign.

This is interesting, but there is though something more important about astrology we need to know! What's new is, we have the technology and the internet! We can get astronomy applied back to astrology.

To understand any change, things need to be explained to the point where you could abandon fear of the unknown, and understand it for yourself.

There is a vast sea of common knowledge diluted down by unaware astrologers and applied ineffectively by popular culture. They are using system of astrology they do not fully understand.

Hopefully as you read on you will gain a good foothold of this knowledge and make the decision for yourse

THE 24° DIFFERENCE

One Simple Fact

Our current system of astrology is aligned with seasonal calendar based on the Sun. It is not aligned with ASTRONOMY. You think it would be easier to actually align it with astronomy! Most people assume that it is. Everyone goes along with whatever the popular system of astrology says.

Once the sun rises, it lights up the sky and we can never really see what constellation it is actually in. There are no stars or planets in the day sky when the sun is out! You do not know what sign the sun is really in unless you check the stars at dawn and sunset. (Or in this day and age, you can refer to a planetarium or sky guide app.) Most people don't even check the credentials of the astrologers, never mind check whats really in the sky.

Like most western astrologers, I was aligned with popular astrology. For a while there I was happy in Tropical zodiac. I was learning about the different ways Astrology worked and that was enough to keep me occupied. Slowly though I began to learn that there was a different system, one that uses true star time. I'd check out this "Sidereal Time" every now and then. After having a Jyotish Reading (astrology from India) I realized something was really different. It set my chart up differently than western. I had different signs and a different chart.

The current popular system follows the path of the sun in the seasonal calendar and applies astronomy to it by turning it 24 degrees back to the first day of spring. It is called Tropical Zodiac.

The one less known, and used in India follows true astronomy and is called Sidereal Time.

So it is, there are two systems in effect being used in astrology. And nobody really knows it or really explains it.

The way I was led into Sidereal Time took time and experience. It kept revealing to me the truth until I understood.

Please read on as I explain these systems for you to understand and draw your own conclusions. I hope your understanding of astrology will grow.

You are more than just your sun sign! You are your entire birth chart.

You are Sidereal Time!

What Sign is the Sun In?

How can you see the constellation
the Sun is in if it is day time?

The skies have been charted, the planets do their orbiting, the Sun does its shining and we on earth live by these repeating cycles. It was the observation of these planets, their energies and patterns to which the ancients applied sensitivity, and the art of Astrology evolved. Whether you believe it works or not, Astrology has been formed thru time and has engrained itself in our society. It is an accepted metaphysical art.

Many people are self taught about the Astrological system by the pop astrology columns in newspapers, books and internet sites. What was once a respected priestly and sacred art, set apart for those that studied and practiced it, is now readily available for casual minds. The true potency of Astrology is hard to find. These days anyone interested can get a casual grasp of this system. There is no official organization to certify astrologers credentials before they can practice.

Look out into a clear night sky and it is unfathomable. The ancients applied a lot of imagination and intuition when they were looking at the sky. Over time they applied a system of order to the stars, it was passed down from culture to culture, and 88 Constellations have become staples. These constellations help organize a very vast sea of stars.

For astrology purposes, the Zodiac is the "circle of animals," that when viewed from here on earth, are behind the path of the Sun. There are twelve main constellations in this path. The Twelve we still use today as our Zodiac, goes back as far as the Babylonians. It is still our astronomical Zodiac.

This is a cosmic thing as well as a scientific thing. Cosmic energies and vibrations that the ancients sensitively observed and experienced became our astrological Zodiac. The descriptions of planets made by these ancient observers are remarkably accurate when compared to modern day technological discoveries.

In my observations I found that the biggest mistake our modern day pop culture astrology is making is this: that few have ever even really looked at the sky and checked where these planets really are. Astronomers know astrology is not correlating with astronomy. This brings even more disdain about the astrology community to them.

People are unwinding with the internet or television at night. Many live where light pollution blocks the full magnificence of the starry night sky. Unless your part astronomer, the vast mystery of the sky remains as such. Many people can spot the big dipper, know a star or two, or thanks to social media, know about the full moons, mercury retrogrades and eclipses. Memes have expanded our social awareness and knowledge of astrology.

Knowing the constellation the Sun is actually is in is a whole other level than just repeating mainstream medias ideas of astrology. You have the power to check to see if astrology is rightly aligned to astronomy.

You may be able to observe just at sunrise or sunset, with faintly visible stars, where the sun really is, but who ever even would think to do this? Check where the sun is? Or would think they even needed to do this? This may be why astrology today does not follow the accurate astronomical placement of stars in the sky. Because no one really can see where the sun is in relation to the zodiac, they take it for granted that the popular system of astrology is using the correct astronomical data.

But with today's technology you don't need to be an astronomer to chart the sky. Personal technology makes this information available for all of us like never before. And this is what is new: Astrologers can now correctly and easily apply correct astronomy thru apps and programs.

The basic fact is: Astrology needs astronomy applied to align to the truth.

The outcome: you may have an Astrology sign identity crisis until you come to understand what Im talking about!

The future outcome: Popular Western astrology actually understands sidereal time and gets correlated.

Why would anyone want a system of astrology that wants to align to the seasons and twist things ahead 24 degrees? To apply the seasons to astrology is not what it is meant for. We do not need to twist astronomy to align to seasons. The seasons and the placement of the stars are two different things. Perhaps it is old fashioned superstition that keeps people in the Tropical system.

I would say the population interested in and applying astrology have never formally explored this subject. Like lemmings following the leader off the cliff, western astrology continues to apply tropical zodiac.

It is just so much more easier and actually accurate to follow true astronomy. It is time to reconsider and reboot our data.

System 1: Tropical Zodiac

"With respect to the Sun and Seasons"

Tropical Zodiac, otherwise known as the system of astrology adopted by "Western" Astrology. It is the system used by popular astrology here in the western world.

It is the Zodiac, placed into the seasonal calendar. The seasons are based on the travel of the earth around the sun. This is a system that links the earths cycle in relation to the travel around the sun. It follows the effects of seasons on the earth. Western astrologers believe that Aries begins with the first breath of spring, March 21, the vernal equinox. This is a poetic alignment, not astronomical. I have interviewed tropical zodiac followers and they are very insistent that astrology needs to be correlated to the seasonal calendar of earth to be correct.

People who have not studied astrology in depth trust the common knowledge about Astrology. I have interviewed a vast number of people and they are all assuming the system they had learned was aligned only to astronomy. Who would ever even question a system that is in use almost everywhere in the western world?

Tropical zodiac isn't all misaligned. True astronomy is applied but then turned back a current 24 degrees. The planets and transits remain in the same pattern and they are just synced back to align the entire zodiac to the Spring Equinox.

Naturally, questions arise. When, where and why did Tropical Zodiac evolve away from Astronomy? Though there are many theories and common sense answers, I cannot find exactly how or why or when or who implemented the change. Time has passed and why it evolved this way is a mystery.

In an upcoming chapter there will be more in depth speculations about this. The hypothesis for the tradition of tropical zodiac being used in Western astrology is possibly connected to the respected knowledge of Ptolemy, a well known astrologer and astronomer in the second century. In the second century Aries was on the rise on the spring equinox and it would have been accurate information. Because his work was so highly regarded just before things happened with the dawn of Christianity, negating most of the astrological culture, his is the last great word on Astrology and Astronomy. Then flash forward 1300 years and Copernicus theory with the Sun being applied at the center of or solar system, people may have thought it practical to apply signs to the seasonal path of the sun. Maybe people were just making it easy, so no one had to get accurate astronomically and they just generalized making the first day of spring is the first day of Aries.

In upcoming chapters I will also explain the precession of the equinox as the earth wobbles a bit and our view of the ever expanding universe actually changes. Even the solar system is moving thru time and space. So to have an astrological calendar date fixed the same year after year, is lacking in common sense. I know people never even thought, why is the astrological calendar fixed if it is an ever changing universe? It is living in fear keeping to a system and being misinformed. And not asking enough questions! Nothing stays the same.

These are the well known dates from the tropical calendar.

TROPICAL ZODIAC:
Aries (March 21-April 19)
Taurus (April 20-May 20)
Gemini (May 21-June 20)
Cancer (June 21-July 22)
Leo (July 23-August 22)
Virgo (August 23-September 22)

Libra (September 23-October 22)
Scorpio (October 23-November 21)
Sagittarius (November 22-December 21)
Capricorn (December 22-January 19)
Aquarius (January 20 to February 18)
Pisces (February 19 to March 20)

The general public is very familiarized with this system. I know this personally because I greet people at my shop and they know their sign, but don't know they are following tropical zodiac.

I know many astrologers are comfortable with this Tropical system. It is what they have learned and apply to their practice. It is a tool they have become well acquainted to working with. Astrological study is endless, and there is always something new to learn and apply. I do think many astrologers might be interested in investigating sidereal time. It is a good day and age to easily see what sidereal time really is. So many people continue on with the Tropical system without even bothering to discover Sidereal time. It is exploring outside our comfort zone where we can grow. Hopefully with the perspectives in this book in the upcoming chapters you can understand this whole subject with an open mind and draw conclusions for yourself.

System 2: Sidereal Zodiac

"Of Or With Respect to the Distant Stars."

This system of astrology is based on true astronomy. It does not alter or adjust itself to meet a seasonal calendar like Tropical zodiac does. It is the actual skies!

Most people assume that Tropical Zodiac is following actual astronomy.

Sidereal time is the system that really follows astronomy.

It is a lesser known system in our culture. There are astrologers that use this system. However It is not being applied in our massive, mass advertised astrological pop culture. It would be a big upheaval, to change calendars. All the astrological trinkets with tropical birth data printed on them would be outdated, and all the people who got their 'sign' tattooed would also be in a bit of a snag.

In Eastern cultures, such as India and Tibet, Sidereal time is the system that is used and has been used since ancient times. Our western culture once had sacred astrological roots, but these were interrupted by the decline of Astrology that came with the rise of Christianity and the Dark Ages. In the East, astrological cultures remain the same, without such a cultural shift. They have always held astrology, the temples, the knowledge and spirituality as a part of their culture.

Sidereal time corresponds to the astronomically correct placement of the constellations. This is the system that takes the alignment from specific, scientifically correct astronomical data. In fact, Sidereal time moves, approximately .75 to 1 degree every century. So to follow the skies, you have to keep adjusting.

Astrology is meant to reflect the energies of the cosmos. And with Sidereal time we get just that, the authentic energies of the planets using correct astronomical data.

Many people assume that popular astrology is accurate. There are often news stories that talk about how the astrological system has had some change. The last chapter discusses the latest 13th sign theory, Ophiuchus, recently popular in the news. But in truth, the news story we need covered is the truth of Sidereal time. This should be whats new about astrology.

The Sidereal system is not completely unknown to modern astrologers. Some astrologers prefer this system over Western Astrology, and are using it in their practice. It is an option in astrological software. It's referred to "Sidereal" or "Lahiri" time in the settings. Back in the 1940s an Astrologer from India by the name of NC Lahiri became known for gaining ground in introducing this system to the West. In technical astrological terms, the astronomical placement in chart data has come to be known as "Lahiri." You can say he is the father of this system being used in the West. In the 1960s and 70's astrologers here in the US and England, were getting hip to the different system, but unfortunately they passed away before getting the knowledge mainstream.

Below are the true sidereal dates. You have the entire rest of the book to breathe and read before you go into shock that your sign may have changed.

SIDEREAL ZODIAC DATES

Aries: April 14 - May 14
Taurus: May 15 - June 14
Gemini: June 15 - July 16
Cancer: July 17 - August 16
Leo: August 17 - September 16
Virgo: September 17 - October 16
Libra: October 17 - November 15
Scorpio: November 16 - December 15
Sagittarius: December 16 - January 14

Capricorn: January 15 - February 13
Aquarius: February 13 - March 14
Pisces: March 15 - April 13

The simple fact is 80% of you have a different sign while 20% remain the same.

Some people adjust easily to Sidereal time. Some people may never care to understand and will stay with Tropical. If you are an old time astrologer and have been studying astrology since you were twelve years old, consider that if you were a twelve year old now, with a smart phone in your hand, you may be actually realizing that astronomy doesn't align to astrology. You would be able to have seen things differently. And if you do have thirty years of using tropical zodiac as your system, I can understand having hard time understanding all this. It does take a little to get used to and I really don't see many people being convinced at first! Give it some time to sink in and to comprehend. Thru my study and observation, I'm totally confident this system vibrates to the truth and brings the true beauty of astrological energies. May you embark on your own journey becoming comfortable and comprehending it's ok to follow the true skies.

In conclusion…..

Tropical zodiac is created by being turned back 24 degrees from actual true astronomical star time to set Aries at sunrise as the first day of spring, on the Equinox. People that use this system are using the notion that astrology should be aligned to the seasonal influence of the earths rotation around the sun.

Aries (March 21-April 19)
Taurus (April 20-May 20)
Gemini (May 21-June 20)
Cancer (June 21-July 22)
Leo (July 23-August 22)
Virgo (August 23-September 22)

Libra (September 23-October 22)
Scorpio (October 23-November 21)
Sagittarius (November 22-December 21)
Capricorn (December 22-January 19)
Aquarius (January 20 to February 18)
Pisces (February 19 to March 20)

Sidereal zodiac is actual true astronomical star time. People that use this system simply align to the true and accurate planetary calculations based on the stars.

SIDEREAL ZODIAC DATES

Aries: April 14 - May 14
Taurus: May 15 - June 14
Gemini: June 15 - July 16
Cancer: July 17 - August 16
Leo: August 17 - September 16
Virgo: September 17 - October 16
Libra: October 17 - November 15
Scorpio: November 16 - December 15
Sagittarius: December 16 - January 14
Capricorn: January 15 - February 13
Aquarius: February 13 - March 14
Pisces: March 15 - April 13

Chapter 2

Learning Thru History

Ptolemy

Copernicus and Galileo

Galileo Quotes

The Astrology of The East: India & Tibet

N. C. Lahiri

The Siderealists

The Hundredth Monkey Effect

Learning Thru History

'There are many systems that have come before in
history that weren't correct, they were so engrained
in the culture it was hard to change them.'

Thru history we can see what happens when engrained systems of thought get challenged. Such as the Earth was once thought to be flat, and also at the center of the solar system, not the sun. Today our topic at hand is that Western astrology currently uses a system of astrology that is not correlated to true astronomy. People assumed thru popular knowledge it is aligned to astronomy.

And there are many other astrologers who knew this, but still don't apply it because it is not easy to go against a well established system. This information should shake your astrological belief system. You may be in shock, and denial. Possibly some people do grasp it right away. I find it takes time and understanding to transition. Similarly, Copernicus defended the theory of how the Sun was at the center of our Solar System. This truth of his understanding challenged the established system of knowledge of the times.

The importance for this book rests on truth seekers and rebels who will deliver the message. Copernicus and Galileo are two such individuals bright enough and strong enough to deliver the truth and go against the conventions of society. The comfort zone and safety of an established theory in use is hard to walk away from. It can take a while for the mass consciousness of society to accept. It was a span of a hundred years that these men had conveying their belief until it took effect.

Ptolemy

Ptolemy was a well known and respected mathematician, astronomer and astrologer who lived in Alexandria in 200AD. He continues to be a well known scholar and figure in history.

One of his series of books, called "The Almagest" is focused on the geo-centric theory, the earth being the center of the solar system. He is well known for his work as it explains in detail the mathematical theory of the motions of the Sun, Moon, and planets.

Also he is known for his work expounding on astrology called the "Tetrabiblos." It is four books and became a very important source book for astrologers for ages to follow. So it could very well be that the astrology is stuck in time with the astronomical calculation of the Spring Equinox from Ptolemy's time.

The dawn of Christianity soon followed and the Roman Empire, a culture once heavily based on Astrology changed its focus. So people interested in Astrology thru the ages could very well look back to his calculations as the last standing astrologer of fame and repute.

If you look back to March 21, 200 AD the Sun was at 1.35 degrees Aries.

Spring equinox aligned with Aries in Ptolemy's day and age! But we now know the view of the skies change over time. Today it is 6 degrees Pisces! So very well his data at the time was correct and perhaps taken as fixed data without astronomical reference being applied.

Though he did have insight into many astrological and scientific matters, he was, in the long run, wrong about the Geocentric theory. Through observation facts were revealed to show the solar centric model to be true.

Nicolaus Copernicus

In the mid 1500s Copernicus was a well respected and studied mathematician and astronomer during Renaissance times. Though traditional perspective had put the EARTH at the center of the Solar System, Copernicus had studied further. The Geo-centric model was the trusted perspective with scholars and institutions was not what Copernicus saw as the truth.

Copernicus, now hailed as the Father of Modern Astronomy declared thru his observation that the SUN, not the EARTH to be the center. This Heliocentrism was not new, it was just not widely supported amongst scholars.

He had to stand his ground as a respected astronomer to maintain this revolutionary scientific point of view. The Renaissance was bringing this truth to the surface. Though it did not become widely accepted in his lifetime, Galileo soon followed Copernicus and tried to promote this heliocentric model.

Indeed it took visionaries and scholars like Copernicus to bring the facts, Galileo to support it and famously take the blame for it, and finally everyone else to catch up and to adapt, and realized the truth, eventually.

Galileo

Galileo was a scholar whose time was just after Copernicus, in the later 1500s. He famously faced political opposition to carry on his belief in the solar-centric model.

At one point in his life, the Church called him a heretic when he agreed with this solar centric theory! Galileo was viewed as a threat and he was placed on house arrest by these authorities of his day. Can you imagine the insult to the conservative people of his time, that an open minded man of learning and reason, challenged the existing structure of knowledge? It's a big deal to decide the Earth is not the center of the things, but the Sun is! Even in this day and age open minded individuals can be received as a problem and cast aside, though they carry the truth.

Here are some quotes from Galileo that can inspire all to become great thinkers:

> "You cannot teach a man anything; you can only help
> him find it within himself."

"All truths are easy to understand once they are discovered; the point is to discover them."

"I do not feel obliged to believe that the same God who has endowed us with sense, reason, and intellect has intended us to forgo their use."

"The sun, with all those planets revolving around it and dependent on it, can still ripen a bunch of grapes as if it had nothing else in the universe to do."

"In questions of science, the authority of a thousand is not worth the humble reasoning of a single individual."

"Measure what is measurable, and make measurable what is not so."

The Astrology of the East:
India and Tibet

It is important to consider other systems of astrology being used in the world today. Tibetan Astrology and Jyotish from India, are both aligned to sidereal time.

"Jyotish" is the name for Indian astrology which means "the science of light." It is a metaphysical art that analyses and forecasts using astronomical data. It helps one to clear their path and remove obstacles thru understanding energies and influences from the past, the present and get a view of timing of events in the future.

It has been developing as far back in cultural history to early civilizations in the Indus Valley.

The planets are considered as deities, and treated as such by astrologers. Sidereal time is honored and applied and has always been the case. The planets are called "NavaGraha" and shrines, temples and priests are still involved with this sacred consideration of astrology.

Tibetan Astrology is engrained with both Jyotish and Chinese astrology. It takes seven years of study to become an astrologer in the Dalai Lamas Institute in Dharmasala. It's a serious profession and helps people with all aspects of life. It uses sidereal time, true astronomy for its calculations.

The impact of astrology on the culture of India and the many holidays is endless. The placement of the moon and sun determine these holy days. The temples follow the astrology and will even close on the day of eclipses, as the light of the eclipse is impure.

There are Holidays such as:

Diwali happens the end of October, early November. It gets celebrated the time of the new moon in the Hindu calendar month of Kartika. The date is every year in the same month, but the day is determined by the moon cycle. It is similar to Easter in Christianity, which is the first Sunday after the full moon of spring.

Deities birthdays such as Lord Krishna, Hanuman and Ganesh are similarly remembered by the calendar month, and moon sign.

Guru Purnima a popular holy day to remember the Guru, falls the first full moon after the summer solstice. Purnima is the name for the full moon phase.

Akshaya Tritiya is celebrated in sidereal Aries. The holiday happens when the sun is exalted, (Aries) and the moon arrives in its exalted sign of Taurus. It's a day of good luck and fortunes, and people use it to marry and magnify blessings.

Makar Sankrati and happens in January as a way to celebrate with the return of the light after winter Solstice. It marks the beginning of longer days as we head towards the Equinox. This holiday isn't dependent on the sun/moon combination but it is a day to celebrate Surya, the Sun and its entrance into Capricorn, under the sidereal time zodiac. It is said that this date was originally aligned to the exact date of Solstice, which Capricorn was once aligned but shifted over time with the precession of the equinoxes or Ayanamsha. These days it is just aligned to the first day of Capricorn as a date marker, which is currently January 15 and not the actual solstice in December.

N.C. Lahiri

NC Lahiri was an Indian Jyotish astrologer and in the 1940s brought his perspective of sidereal time to western popular culture. The gap or difference in times between the Eastern zodiac and the Western zodiac would be very obvious to anyone with a back ground in this astrology from India. He is known for popularizing Ayanamsha. It is the Sanskrit term in Indian astronomy for the amount of precession. In astrology, this is the longitudinal difference between the Tropical and Sidereal zodiacs. He borrowed this from its inventors the Ketkar Brothers who propounded this idea three decades before him.

Basically, Lahiri brought western astrology the awareness of the true alignment of astronomy to astrology. Today, if you look in your western astrology program it can be referred to as "sidereal," "ayanamsa" and/or "Lahiri."

In the astrology of India, 'Sayana Chakra' is Tropical Zodiac and 'Nirayana Chakra' is Sidereal Zodiac. Sayana is based on the Vernal Equinox and Sidereal time is based on the fixed stars.

There is a current Lahiri-Ayanamsa ephemeris that was founded by late N. C. Lahiri in 1939, the first Indian member of the Ephemerides-Commission of the International Astronomical Union, Paris, and the first Officer-in-charge of the then Nautical Almanac Unit of the Govt. of India, now known as Positional Astronomy Centre at Kolkata. This ephemeris is intended to provide most accurate and up-to-date astronomical data in advance to its users.

The ephemeris is based on Nirayana or sidereal system of

calculation. It established Spica as a fixed star, to determine star time. Astrologers would use these books called "ephemeris" which were filled with astrological data for each and ever day going back 100 years and ahead as well. You could draw a chart up from these books. But nowadays the computer programs hold the ephemeris and calculate the charts saving much time. Finding astronomical data is a snap.

The "Siderealists"

The 1960s brought a wave of astrologers aware of sidereal time. The Irish astrologer Cyril Fagan began the modern "Siderealist" tradition in the late 1940s. He supported the role of fixed stars in the establishment of the zodiacal framework. Many like him were creating the movement but it faded out with their deaths in the 1970s.

The Hundredth Monkey Effect

In the early 1950s Scientists were conducting observations with a group of macaque monkeys on an island in Japan. They noticed that some monkeys had learned to wash sweet potatoes before they ate them. Gradually the younger generation caught on thru observation and repetition. The conclusion was that once a critical number of monkeys was reached, "The Hundredth Monkey," the previously unknown behavior spread instantly to other monkeys across the water and on nearby islands.

This creates a graceful opportunity for the spread of useful new ideas.

However, over time accurate information can sometimes be misrepresented as well. Perhaps this is what happened to cause us to go off course from using true astronomy. Hopefully this effect can reverse the mis information and help create some change to bring sidereal time quickly to the top

Chapter 3

The Ever Changing Skies

The Precession of Equinoxes

Dawning of the Age of Aquarius

The 24 Degree Adjustment

Tropical Zodiac Dates

Sidereal Zodiac Dates

The Percentages

The 24 Day Difference

Planetarium App Experiment

The Ever Changing Skies

Everything changes. Nothing remains the same. Songs have been written about it, books are filled with heartbreaking poems, we all know time keeps moving on. This is an ever changing universe.

If we apply this reality to tropical zodiac, then there is no way any astral body could hold still forever more. It is nonsense that Aries would align to the first day of spring every year. It is a mere poetic adjustment, not an actual astronomical one. Most people I've talked to are surprised to find that Tropical zodiac, the name for the system they use, (many people aren't aware there is a choice of which system they use), is not aligned to astronomy. They think they are using an accurate astronomy in their astrology. But there is a choice.

If you were to observe in this current year what sign the Sun rises in on the Vernal Equinox, the first day of spring, March 21, you would be viewing it (in 2018) as an astronomically correct 6 degrees Pisces. Traditionally accepted Tropical zodiac forcefully turns back Aries to March 21, year, after year, after year. Sidereal time you will see the Sun not in the first degree of Aries, but naturally in flux and currently at 6 degrees Pisces.

The question that should arise is, why is it that the zodiac does not actually appear to be stable? ...

The Precession of Equinoxes

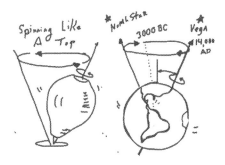

The motion of all things in this universe is a constant. We mostly take it for granted that our Earth Mother is spinning at 1600mph. Her spinning is creating the Sunrise and Sunset. She creates the day and the night.

The Earth's speed around the orbit of the Sun is said to be 67,000mph. And when you apply that our solar system itself is in motion at 514,000 mph, how can you even sleep at night?

To add to all this crazy motion, you may or may not remember from school this other fact. The Earth wobbles! Every hundred years we actually are shifting backward a degree of our orientation to the skies.

So to chart real astrology you really have to keep track things with astronomy. It also might be why somewhere along the line someone said the heck with it, it is too much to keep up with. Lets just simplify it and put Aries as the first day of spring so we don't have to keep track of all this stuff!

In our modern times with technology, computers are doing the work for us and it is easy to get to true astronomy.

Here is the recent movement caused by the wiggle:

March 21,2000 - Sun is 7.16 Pisces.
March 21,2015 - Sun is 7.2 Pisces.
March 21,2017 - Sun is 6:53 Pisces.

As you can see there is a slight shift backward in signs every year. It is an additive wobble changing slowly but significantly up to a degree approximately every 71.5 years. Due to the slight wobble in the earth, every year we shift a bit and the view changes. Though it may be that the universe is also expanding and shifting it is too subtle in our small time frame to tell. But the wobble is detectable and it is known to science as the "Precession of the Equinox," or in Sanskrit terms, another popular name for it is, Ayanamsha.

Back in the BC, in ancient cultures like Babylonia, where astrology was held sacred, and Astrologers were priests in temples, there is a good chance they were accurately following the sky. The literal charting of the exact positions of the sky would reveal them the most information.

In the Roman culture astrology was deeply engrained in their culture. You can see it is still standing in architecture and in the root of their language. But as the Roman Empire converted deeper to Christianity, so we begin to see this Piscean age on the rise. While the Roman Empire was building towards unifying under Christ, so the cultures sacred connection to Astrology was being left behind.

The Roman culture and calendar was loaded with astronomical and astrological references. The further Christianity advanced, the less that astrology was at the center of culture. So clearly we are living "stuck" back in the age of "Aries" if we continue to live by this system of Tropical Zodiac. The Age of Christ even correlates to "the Fishes," and here with Sidereal time we see Pisces starting on the rise on Spring Equinox by 500AD.

March 21, 001 AD Sun is 2. 15 Aries
March 21, 100 AD Sun is 2.13 Aries
March 21, 200 AD Sun is 1.35 Aries
March 21, 300 AD Sun is 0.56 Aries
March 21, 400 AD Sun is 0.17 Aries
March 21, 500 AD Sun is 29.39 Pisces
March 21, 600 AD Sun in 29.1 Pisces
March 21, 700 AD Sun in 28.22 Pisces
March 21, 800 AD Sun in 27.44 Pisces
March 21, 900 AD Sun in 27.6 Pisces
March 21, 1000AD Sun in 26 28 Pisces
March 21, 1100AD Sun in 25.50 Pisces
March 21, 1200 AD Sun in 25.12 Pisces
March 21, 1300AD sun in 24.33 Pisces
March 21, 1400 AD Sun in 23.55 Pisces
March 21, 1500 AD Sun in 23.17 Pisces

Dawning of the Age of Aquarius

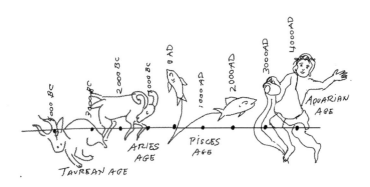

We have heard this phrase many times. It was born into spiritual pop culture in the 1960s by the popular song "Aquarius/Let the Sun Shine In" from the musical "Hair."

What does this "Dawning of the Age of Aquarius" mean and where does it get its name? There has been many "ages" in civilization and these are heralded in by the degree of the rising sign on the vernal equinox. Simply put, the sign on the rise the first day of spring at sunrise represents the "age" of the time.

It is said we are entering the Age of Aquarius. In fact the sign rising is currently at 6 degrees Pisces, and moving towards Aquarius. So we still have 6 degrees to get to Aquarius! But have no fear. The star clusters behind those 6 degrees of Pisces lean more towards social change and uniting of people, so it has dawned!

If our astrological calendar is aligned to Tropical zodiac, then we are still in the Aries age! Folks, the Age of Aquarius is dawning, and this a big reason to start waking up to the astronomical alignment of Sidereal time. Tropical zodiac, and its application of Aries being on the rise in its first degree, is really aligning time back before the birth of Christ. If you check the calendars back in time, you can see that Christ was born as a catalyst in the final centuries of the Aries age, just before the Piscean age began. In true astronomy, we are now in the end of the Piscean age. The age of Aquarius officially starts 2600AD.

So give it a couple hundred years, humanity is still working things out!

Here is a data list of precession of the equinox into the future:

March 21, 1900 AD - Sun is 7.56 Pisces.
March 21, 2000 AD - Sun is 7.16 Pisces.
March 21, 2015 AD - Sun is 7.2 Pisces.
March 21, 2017 AD Sun is 6:53 Pisces
March 21, 2050 AD Sun is at 6:25 Pisces
March 21, 2100 AD Sun is at 5:39 Pisces
March 21, 2200 AD Sun at 4:1 Pisces
March 21, 2300 AD Sun at 2:23 Pisces
March 21, 2400 AD Sun at 1:45 Pisces
March 21, 2500 AD Sun at 00:7 Pisces
March 21, 2600 AD Sun at 28:29 Aquarius

It is easy to see in the chart above that the degree of the sun moves back a degree or so every century.

This precession or 'wobble,' along with the eccentricity in the orbit of the earth, is causing this shift. In the day of Ptolemy, in the second century, people thought the earth was at the center everything, so without observation would know the skies were changing. So to truly follow astronomy, an astrologer would have to be aware of and keep track of this kind of transition. Who knows if they knew a wiggle caused it or not.

So shifting and adjusting to a different system is not a mystery, and we can easily shift adjust to true sidereal time with modern technology doing the work for us.

True astrology is not locked in a constant given time frame of a seasonal calendar, but one that is organically moving in space and time. In Jyotish, the astrology from India, Tibetan Astrology, and other Eastern Astrology, this has been the uninterrupted case for astrology. They keep adjusting their data to what is currently in the sky.

So too the Earth is having changes here at the end of the Piscean age, and we are merely at the Dawn of this new time. So, somebody, please, lets get this calendar aligned and so that we all can see clearly: we are on the brink of changing the world for the better: ideas of a supportive unity for all on the planet are not far fetched, they are just beginning to take root.

The 24 Degree Difference

The Ayanamsa: Comparing the Gap of Tropical to Sidereal

If we compare these two systems, we discover that the popular system of Tropical Zodiac is actually 23.7 degrees as of 2108 off from what is actually in the sky astronomically. But for the ease of learning, it is averaged out to 24 degrees. You might think this is crazy due the fact we are going for truth and accuracy, but in this, you can see how easily any "little adjustment for ease of learning" might have taken hold.

People who have come to know and love their sign may be surprised they have a different sign than what they thought they had. But this 'new' sign is the sign that holds the astronomical truth about where the Sun really was when you were born.

Tropical Zodiac puts the Sun in Aries at 0 degrees on the Equinox.

Sidereal Zodiac currently sees the Sun at 6 degrees Pisces. Do the math, it is a 24 degree difference!

SUN ENTERS ARIES:

TROPICAL Zodiac

JAN	FEB	MARCH (21)
APRIL	MAY	JUNE
JULY	AUGUST	SEPTEMBER
OCT	NOV	DEC

APPLYS MARCH 21 AS THE FIRST DAY OF ARIES

SIDEREAL Zodiac

JAN	FEB	MARCH
APRIL (14)	MAY	JUNE
JULY	AUGUST	SEPT
OCT	NOV	DEC

FOLLOWS WHAT IS ACTUALLY IN THE CURRENT SKY

At this point in the book we have established these basic facts. Tropical Zodiac keeps March 21 as a constant for the start of the zodiac. It takes the actual astronomy of the skies but turns it back 24 degrees to fit this grid system of dates, which puts the Sun in Aries at 0 degrees on the Equinox.

Like a giant wheel, they take the heavens and all the placements of planets, stars, Sun and Moon, and turn it back from April 14 to March 21. They make it align with the first day of spring. It is a very poetic adjustment.

TROPICAL ZODIAC DATES

Aries (March 21-April 19)
Taurus (April 20-May 20)
Gemini May 21-June 20)
Cancer (June 21-July 22)
Leo (July 23-August 22)
Virgo (August 23-September 22)
Libra (September 23-October 22)
Scorpio (October 23-November 21)
Sagittarius (November 22-December 21)
Capricorn (December 22-January 19)
Aquarius (January 20 to February 18)
Pisces (February 19 to March 20)

Sidereal Zodiac is where the Sun currently and actually is: 6 Pisces on the equinox. The sidereal calendar correlates astronomically to the heavens.

SIDEREAL ZODIAC DATES

Aries: April 14 - May 14
Taurus: May 15 - June 14
Gemini: June 15 - July 16
Cancer: July 17 - August 16
Leo: August 17 - September 16
Virgo: September 17 - October 16

Libra: October 17 - November 15
Scorpio: November 16 - December 15
Sagittarius: December 16 - January 14
Capricorn: January 15 - February 13
Aquarius: February 13 - March 14
Pisces: March 15 - April 13

Considering the changes in percentages it seems quite a dramatic 24 degree difference. Not just Aries is 24 degrees back, but every sign, every planet, every birth chart rising sign is 24 degrees back.

The 24 Day Difference

To further understand the calendar shift, we can envision the following:

The complete 360 degree rotation of the earth around the Sun takes 365 days.

There are 12 months in the year with approximately 30 days per month.

The zodiac is behind that rotation with its 360 degree full circle.

There are 12 signs in the Zodiac with approximately 30 degrees in each sign.

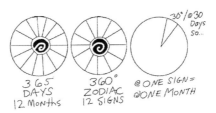

The Sun moves approximately one degree every day. If we assign days to degrees, this gives us approximately one degree a day or 30 Days per sign.

We can easily exchange days and degrees, and can conclude that Tropical and Sidereal Zodiac have a 24 degree, or 24 Day difference.

The remaining 6 Days are actually in an overlap, and remain are the same for both systems.

So it is that Tropical Zodiac turns astronomy, like a wheel, 24 degrees back until Aries aligns with March 21. Sidereal time just uses it where it is.

The Percentages

This works out to be, in mathematical terms, a 24 degree adjustment from tropical. 80% of you have a different sign than what you thought you had. 20% of the people are in an overlap with the same sign they thought they had. This is a BIG difference!

It would break down as follows:

30 days per sign
24 Days back
6 Days remain the same.
6 goes into 30 five times.
To convert to percent we put things at 100, so 1/5, or
6 days is 20%, leaving 80% as the 24 days.

So we can say in percentages:

80% have a different sign than what they thought they had.
20% of the people are holding the same sign they thought they had.

You may need resuscitation after this.

If your sign is in the 80%, you will have a different sign than prescribed previously, but before you run into a panic that your sign changed, check the following chapters. As there is always some new perspective to learn in astrology, you might find the information that is being presented will help you deeper understand astrology as well helping integrate this new alignment. It will help you understand better even what a "sign" is. If you are in the 20% and your sign remains the same, you can still check in and hopefully gain some new insight

The Experiment

You can't see what sign the Sun is in by looking at it during the day (duh)! It is the simple fact that not only leaves the blind following the blind in Tropical zodiac, but can leave you blind! If you have a smart phone, go to your App Store and search for a planetarium app. Once uploaded check out where the sun is. Note what constellation it is in. Then, check out the two calendars, where is the sun and where is the sun supposed to be? You should notice a distinct gap in actual placement of the two systems.

Take a deep breath and let it sink in. Astrology depends on energies, feeling and not just data. When you see this actual difference, how does it affect you?

Another way to understand the difference is to take a look where the sun actually is on your next birthday. Have you ever even checked the sky on your birthday to see what sign you actually have?

Chapter 4

Transitioning to the Sidereal System

A Better Understanding of Astrology

What is a Sun sign?

The Rising Sign

The Houses

The Moon

Planetary Rulers

Your Sidereal Sign

Planetary Transits

Intuitive Astrology: The Metaphysical Science

Following the Moon: Experiment

Transitioning to the
Sidereal System

I have found many people have "mis-diagnosed" themselves with astrology.

Being misdirected to the wrong sign, has also happened to me. It is happening to you, and it is happening to almost everybody! People have 'self-prescribed!' a sign seeing the tropical zodiac system calendar, and adopted all its attributes to suit themselves. It is my perspective that there are a lot of people, almost everybody, using astrology casually but not correctly.

Just as people go to web medical sites for self diagnosis, people go to astrology sites and diagnose themselves. You may get some information and knowledge from it, but how do you know your getting accurate information? If you feel pain in your heal when you walk, are you better off going to a Podiatrist and getting an MRI, and a doctors experience to access the problem, or to a medical website and trying to understand the whole of podiatry to diagnose yourself? With a doctors experience and professional tests, you have good chances of being properly assessed and will know how to best heal your problem. This is how Astrology is. It needs to be taken as seriously as a medical art. You can dabble in it, but to truly study it and practice it leads to different levels of understanding.

The study of any subject can be compared to riding a bike. At first you know you want to be bike riding, but you need practice. You may need training wheels. Using pop culture astrology, no one really gets past training wheels. The sidereal system will be like going from training wheels to a racing bike for some. You may not be comfortable with it at first and need to gain balance and courage. So hopefully the upcoming chapter will bring some basic understanding of astrology will be the training wheels you need to get the courage to grasp and use true astronomy sidereal time. You will be riding with all the best equipment and will be in fine shape!

A Better Understanding
of Astrology

What exactly is Your "SIGN"?

I'd like to address this most basic and obvious observation. This is the base foundation of Western Astrology everyone knows from years of exposure to popular astrology. But lets take a closer look.

What is a Sun sign? In this chapter to know what a "sun sign" is, is our goal. To best understand what our sign is we need to first grasp the basics and understand what the sun represents.

Then once people find out what sign they are, they become attached to that sign. From the day you assign yourself your sun sign, it became increasingly engrained in you. Then years pass. You and your sign are one. You may even find you follow an astrology website that also uses this system, and it further reinforces the system. Then you talk about astrology with other people who have the tropical system engrained from their repeat exposure of it and so it all seems valid.

All along you and your friends assumed ASTROLOGY WAS FOLLOWING ASTRONOMY. There now…you might be feeling slightly off, or maybe your interested how your engrained belief system of astrology could be challenged by another system. Is it true? Is it right, what the heck is it?

In this chapter we are going to look a little further into astrology to broaden the horizons of understanding. We are more than just our sun sign diagnosis. Many people use it as if it is all that they are represented by astrology.

I assure you have an entire universe at your demand, not just a sun sign.

The Sun

Your SUN SIGN is IMPORTANT
but so are the other planets!

The Sun is pure energy and light. It is not a planet at all, but a star. An incredibly mystical and amazing mass of energy that sustains our solar system! So it is an important influence when considering a persons chart. It is the source of life.

In a chart it holds its powerful presence in a particular spot of the sky. It reveals our source essence of self. It is pure expression of the soul. It stands strong in a chart as the individuals main influence. Planets near by and in relation to it can lend their influence. The sun can also reveal information about the father manifested in this life and the relationship with him.

Since the zodiac fits so neatly into the calendar, by knowing the day you were born, people can easily look at the assigned dates, apply their birthday, and see their sun sign. But that is not looking at the sky to 'see' what sign the Sun really is in on their birthday. It was just by following the tropical calendar of dates one applied their birthdate and followed Astrology. You never knew if you were following Tropical Zodiac or Sidereal Zodiac.

The Sun sign is important but not 'stand alone' significant as all the advertisements and horoscopes make it out to be.

It is a simple and friendly way to discuss astrology. It is a social novelty more than the whole truth of any individuals chart.

The Ruling Planet

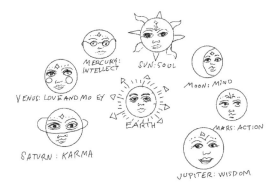

The simplest way to understand your sun sign is to understand its assigned "ruler." This planetary ruler holds the key that best describes the energy your sign has. It is a short cut that helps you understand the twelve zodiac signs.

Every planet in its ruler is strong. Each planet has a sign where it is exalted, and feels content. Each planet has a sign where it feels uncomfortable and struggles to express itself.

Our charts are filled with planets that are weak, strong and neutral.

And depending on where they are in the sky, the degree of the sign they are in, they can gain and lose strength.

So if you include your Sun sign, and apply its ruler, then you start to paint the picture of what your sign has to offer!

And to get more in depth, read ahead to the Rising sign, Moon sign and other planets and their relation to the sun and each other further explain the cosmic mystery that you are. It is the time of birth that determines this exact position they are in your chart. Knowing this birth information helps astrology assess the living chart of the unique essence that is you.

Here are the planets and their rulers:

The Sun is the ruler of Leo. It represents the Soul and sense of self. It is exalted in Aries and detriment Libra.

The Moon is the ruler of Cancer. It represents emotions, the Mind. It is exalted in Taurus and detriment Scorpio.

Mercury is the ruler of Gemini, and of Virgo. It represents intelligence and communication. It is exalted in Virgo and detriment in Pisces.

Mars is the ruler of Aries and Scorpio. It represents action, courage and energy. It is exalted in Capricorn and detriment in Cancer.

Venus is the ruler of Taurus and Libra. It represents relationships, art and pleasures. It is exalted in Pisces and detriment in Virgo.

Jupiter is the ruler of Sagittarius and Pisces(Indian Astrology). It brings opportunity, optimism and wisdom. It is Exalted in Cancer and detriment in Capricorn.

Saturn is the ruler of Capricorn and Aquarius(using Indian Astrology). It represents responsibility and reality. It is exalted in Libra and detriment in Aries.

The Moon

The Moon is a very important part of the chart best determined by time of birth. It moves through a sign every two and half days. The moon represents our mind. It shows how we are wired emotionally.

The planets in the moons company can influence the mind. The moon on the rise can reveal an individual with much intuition and sensitivity. A setting moon shows someone interested in having many friends as a support system. A moon with Mars shows a quick temper, and the moon with Jupiter shows someone who is optimistic.

In Jyotish, the astrology from India, the moon is as big a player as the sun and the rising sign. Much information gets revealed from the degree of the moon. The Dasha system is a system of prediction in Jyotish that is set by the degree of the moon at birth using the rising sign. It reveals planetary time periods that help shape our lives. The star cluster the moon is placed in is called a Nakshatra and is a vital part of understanding the individual. There are 27 Nakshatra's or stations of the moon, a very subtle and exacting system that reveals much information.

The moon itself shows our emotional tendencies and sensitivity. It is a window to understand the kind of Mother we have manifested here in Earth life and our relationship with her. The three most important keys to a chart is the Rising sign, the Sun sign and the Moon sign. This is basic first layer of information an astrologer considers when viewing an individual chart.

The Rising Sign

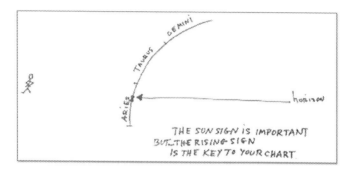

The zodiac sign that was on the horizon the day, time and place you were born is the rising sign. This "rising sign" holds the energy of our first breath at birth. It is the most important feature in a chart, more than the Sun sign.

To obtain the knowledge of the rising sign compared to that of the sun sign involves knowing the birth time. The sun sign simply fits easily into our calendar. Basic sun sign information is easily obtained in popular websites, apps and magazine columns. Applying your birth time and place of birth requires an extra step not as easily accessed in mainstream information.

The rising sign is the true key to ones birth chart, determined by the birth time of an individual. The time of birth determines what was on the rise when you were born. It is also the key revealing the placement of the Sun and the planets. The rising sign holds much information as to what animates an individual. It is the person we see walking in the room. It is with the rising sign with which we first took our first breath. It is strong hit of energy.

A sign is a series of stars. These stars, or constellation, when you feel into it holds a certain energy. The sign and possible planets and stars on the rise can tell much about who we are. In India, when they say, "Whats your sign?" they are asking for the rising sign, not your sun sign!

The Chart: Understanding The Houses

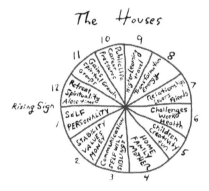

The chart is determined by the rising sign. It sets the layout as to what the rulers of each "house" is. The planets and what houses they fall in tells much about the energy of an individual. Life path timing of events, graces and even obstacles are seen. The houses where planets fall reveal the areas where you have work to do. Your strengths and weakness are built right in for you to manage and work with. The energy points in a chart are subtle and endless. So it is rather ridiculous to put so much stress and influence on just a sun sign.

The chart is the zodiac thumbprint of energy that we are born with. It becomes a matrix describing our energies and potentials. It is a blueprint for the soul. The placement of the Sun and planets within this Zodiac reveal your essence. The Sun and planets take on an other layer of information as they are formed in character with the house they fall in. Using this 12 house system, each house represents a different aspect of life.

1st House: the Self, personality
2nd House : stability, family, values, money
3rd House: self will, communication, siblings, neighbors
4th House: Home, Family, Mother
5th House: Children, creativity
6th House: Challenges, Work, Health
7th House : Relationships, Helpful People
8th House: Transformation, Energies
9th House: Higher Learning, Gurus, Travel
10th House: Public Life, Career
11th House: Gains, Spiritual Growth, Groups
12th House: Spirituality, Retreat,

Transits

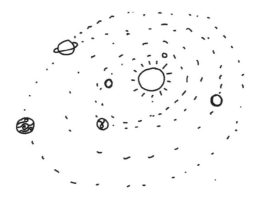

These are current planetary forces that are effecting you. Everyday the cosmic forces are moving and creating different energy patterns and affecting us on multiple levels. In a reading they are aligned to our chart and birth planets to see how they are influencing us personally in this vast cosmic sea of energy.

Planets not only move direct, but with the timing of orbits can appear to move backwards as well. While all this clockwork of planetary motion is occuring, we are all influenced by the relations these planets are having with each other and our own interior energies.

While direct motion can litereally help us move ahead, retrogrades can bring in a holding period and review time.

Applying this planetary movement to our sun sign and charts, you can see how much influence we are under every day. There are so many changes.

Transits can help us understand the timing of events. When

applied, they can be very helpful as a prediction tool. This brings awareness that things take time. You do have, some times of good fortune and some times of delay.

We are not just influenced by our Sun sign, chart and birth planets, but we are daily under the influence of current planets and their movements.

Here is how much planetary movement is going on everyday:

The Sun travels about 1 degree per day and spends approximately 30 days in each sign.

The Moon goes through all twelve signs about every 28 days. It spends approximately 2 1/2 days in each sign.

Mercury takes approximately one year to go through all of the twelve signs. Mercury can stay in one sign from about 14 to 30 days, depending on its motion.

Venus travels up to a degree a day, depending on its motion, and stays in a sign approximately 23 days to a little over 2 months (Every 8 years it returns to the same degree and over time forms the pentagram—).

Mars travels up to a degree per day depending on its motion, and takes about 2 years to go through all 12 signs, staying in one sign for about 1.5 months.

Jupiter takes about 12 years to go through the 12 signs, staying in one sign an average of one year. Jupiter travels from 0 to 14 minutes of a degree a day depending on whether it is retrograde or in direct motion.

Saturn travels from 0 to 8 minutes of a degree per day depending on its motion and takes approximately 29 1/2 years to go through all twelve signs, staying in one sign for about 2 1/2 years.

Uranus travels from 0 to 4 minutes of a degree per day, depending on its motion and it moves through all twelve signs of the Zodiac in approximately 84 years, staying in one sign about 7 years.

Neptune travels from 0 degrees to 3 minutes of a degree per day, depending on its motion. It takes Neptune about 165 years to go through all 12 signs, staying in each one for approximately 14 years.

Pluto travels from 0 to three minutes of a degree a day and takes approximately 248 years to go through all 12 signs, staying in each one from 14 to 30 years.

Your Sun sign is affected by the Rising Sign, which determines what house it is in. The Moon, the planetary ruler, current transits, all tell the story of you, which is way more than just what a "sun sign" has to offer. All these influences are a map of the cosmic mystery that you are.

To everything (turn, turn, turn)
There is a season (turn, turn, turn)
And a time to every purpose, under heaven
A time to be born, a time to die
A time to plant, a time to reap
A time to kill, a time to heal
A time to laugh, a time to weep...

Pete Seeger/ The Byrds

The Intuitive Art of Astrology

What is METAPHYSICAL?

Miriam Webster dictionary explains metaphysical as

"of or relating to the transcendent or to a reality beyond what is perceptible to the senses fleeing from experience to a metaphysical realm" — John Dewey

"supernatural fate and metaphysical aid doth seem to have thee crown'd" — William Shakespeare

What is Transcendent?
Beyond or above the range of normal or merely physical human experience.

"The search for a transcendent level of knowledge" (of God) existing apart from and not subject to the limitations of the material universe.

Synonyms:

mystical, mystic, transcendental, spiritual, divine; metaphysical "the search for a transcendent level of knowledge"

Astrology is a Metaphysical science. It is something we need to transcend our normal daily activity to feel into. It is happening in every second and the second in-between time. It is affecting our energy. On a physical level we are made up of thousands of energy receptors. Add to that our bodies are composed of 60% water. In the center of this is what we really are, the soul. So we are excellent conductors of the cosmic energies. It is with this that we feel, intuit and act. We are influenced when these "nadis" or energy points are effected by cosmic energies. This is why understanding and applying true Sidereal time in Astrology is so important.

Many people simply are unaware of our true potential. They are walking around unconscious to these forces. They basically are blocking and ignoring the very force that they are. It is a gift to be alive, and it so extraordinary that everyone reacts and deals with their own individual way.

If you want to experience this quality of astrology than I would recommend you to first ask yourself, are you open to sitting and feeling into these divine energies? Maybe you already are.

One way to experiment with the 'vibes' from astrology would be to keep track of the moons transit. Once again, as I stated earlier a good tool for following the suns transit is with a sky guide app, so you will best off with a Moon app or sky guide that follows sidereal time.

A good experiment would be to use a Moon app that has sidereal and tropical time and compare tropical to sidereal moon sign placements to see what feels more true.

The moon is the closest influence to the earth. It also changes rapidly thru signs, taking a two and a half days approximately in each sign. As it transits thru the signs you may begin to intuitively feel the experience of the moon and the sign it is in. Check in how you feel and what other people act like. Note experiences you have during the day. Then check to see what the ruler of the moon is and what planets it is with.

In India, Jyotish astrology has 27 Nakshatra's, or stations of the moon. So it is a very sensitive system feeling into 27 star clusters that reside in the 12 zodiac system.

I have noticed, for example it is much easier to have fun when the moon is Leo, and wait to organize when the moon is in Virgo. If the moon is in Scorpio I understand why reality may be feeling kind of heavy. When we move from a Pisces moon to an Aries moon I notice the shift in energy from ethereal to action. So it is that the ancient ones sat in harmony with the earth and sky and connected in and charted our system of astrology.

Astrology formed slowly over time. It was passed down formally thru transmission from teacher to student. It evolved thru the ages and when it started following a seasonal calendar and not an astronomical one, is hard to know.

It has been seen thru time how many kings have changed things in the kingdom when it comes under their rule. Such as the King James version of the Bible! So it may be that astrologers unknown, at some point in the past, with the rise of Christianity and decline of Roman culture, decided on this tropical system.

For us to truly to feel the essence of the planetary movements, we need to be in synch with their actual location. Only then are we using real astrology.

Chapter 5

What's Your New Sun Sign?

Rethinking the Zodiac Signs

Aries
Taurus
Gemini
Cancer
Leo
Virgo
Libra
Scorpio
Sagittarius
Capricorn
Aquarius
Pisces

Sidenote: Ophicius

What's Your Sun Sign?
Rethinking the Zodiac Signs

If you have read thru the book this far, you know that there are two systems of astrology.

Back in the previous chapters we figured that since there is 30 degrees in each sign, and that popular mainstream tropical zodiac currently turns back astronomy 24 degrees, it would be that in each sign 24 days have a different sign, but 6 days remain in a gap with the same sign.

We further explained in the previous chapters that many people may have had a limited education on astrology and are misdiagnosing themselves. The study of astrology is endless and one need to keep gaining in knowledge and understanding.

It is best to have an open mind and try different principles.

"Whats your sign?" Virtually means nothing to an astrologer. It reveals some, but not everything about your character. An astrologer relies on your birth time, birthdate and birthplace. These three elements set the stage for full completion of a "chart."

The following is a more integrated description of the twelve zodiac signs, followed by celebrities with the sun sign, and then one example of a celebrity birth chart. More than their sun signs, we get a broader story from the "chart". Hopefully this will help your understanding of sidereal time applied to your chart, then you will then truly understand the planets and the energies they reveal.

As mentioned earlier in the book, when you observe the planetarium app test, you see that the planets are really in a different sign than what the tropical zodiac calendar states. When you see it with your very own eyes...what will you do? Are you going to sit there and just keep following an old system or you will you question it? Will you have the guts to say OK - I'm ready for this exciting adjustment the system of astrology needs? Will there become a demand for Sidereal based astrology? So please check the skies for true astronomy, and let's start a revolution.

In the next chapter, since most people are familiar with popular astrology's use of the sun sign system, I will apply it here to help get a better understanding of the shift. These translations of the basics of the signs spoon feeds you about your Sun sign in the new system, but I want you to remember the sun sign is not the only sign you are.

You are your rising sign, your moon sign, and all the signs your Mercury, Venus, Mars, Jupiter, Saturn, Uranus Neptune and Pluto are placed in. And their house placements and relationships to one another tell even more of the story. There are so many layers to be considered in a chart, it is a multi dimensional soul print of who you are.

As a side note, please read up on the "13th" sign after this chapter.

Your "New" Sign!
The 12 Zodiac Signs

SIDEREAL ZODIAC DATES
Aries: April 14 - May 14
Taurus: May 15 - June 14
Gemini: June 15 - July 16
Cancer: July 17 - August 16
Leo: August 17 - September 16
Virgo: September 17 - October 16
Libra: October 17 - November 15
Scorpio: November 16 - December 15
Sagittarius: December 16 - January 14
Capricorn: January 15 - February 13
Aquarius: February 13 - March 14
Pisces: March 15 - April 13

80% of you may have a different sign than what you previously learned.
The other 20% remain the same.

Aries

April 14 - May 14

Element: Fire
Ruled by Mars
Color: Red
Gemstone: Red Coral
Body: The Head

Yes, people, we start the zodiac year with Aries, and it is a great start as we have plenty of energy with Mars bringing in the fire element getting things underway. This is the first sign in the zodiac bringing bright youthfulness to the soul here.

Fresh energy, action taking, strength and vigor are all here when considering Aries. Importantly, the Sun is exalted here. This gives Aries people a good sense of themselves. They need understand who they are, and a sense of 'Who am I' and 'What am I' doing is very strong. It's not a "Stubborn Taurus" but an "Independent Aries" situation. The ruling planet Mars makes them people that take action and do things. They can play a helping role, and be there to serve. They can be medical workers and healers. A quick and alert call to action can make them excellent caretakers. They are Shamanistic and can shift energy thru their dynamic power.

Though they are service oriented, they remain independent. Independence is a strong theme for this sign, as having the space to do what they need to when they have to do it, can look selfish, but really they are acting out as leaders. They are driven to do what they feel they need to do.

Mars as the ruling planet can bring in direct action, which can be viewed as, a lack of compromise and sometimes conflict in relationships. They are usually spartan and efficient, and not too far out on the luxury side.

If you thought you were a Taurus and now find your self diagnosed as an Aries:

The good news is, with the Sun here in Aries, you have an Exalted Sun sign and a good sense of yourself. You are a leader. But remember, you could have other planets in Taurus, so this sun sign description is only part of the story.

Aries is ruled by Mars. So when Mars is in the sign of Aries, it brings strength, drive and a strong constitution to the chart.

Aries Sun People:

Emma Watson - April 15
Charlie Chaplin - April 16
Victoria Beckham - April 17
Jennifer Garner - April 17
Kourtney Kardashian - April 18
James Franco - April 19
Kate Hudson - April 19
Miranda Kerr - April 20
Queen Elizabeth - April 21
Jack Nicholson - April 22
Al Pacino - April 25
Uma Thurman - April 29
David Beckham - May 2
Audrey Hepburn - May 4
Adele - May 5
George Clooney - May 6
Katherine Hepburn - May 12
Robert Patterson May 13

Aries Chart Study

Audrey Hepburn
May 4, 1929
Ixelles, Belgium
3:00am
Rising Sign: Aquarius
Sun Sign: Aries
Moon: Aquarius

Audrey Hepburn is a famous actress and model from 1950s and 1960s.

Her famous roles came from being an impetuous youthful, independent thinking woman.

Her character Holly, in Breakfast at Tiffany's and Eliza Doolittle, in My Fair Lady were perfectly suited to her chart.

Audreys sidereal time Sun was in Aries, in the company of Jupiter and the North Node. This North Node showed she needed to think of herself in this life, and though she had relationships, she had to put herself first and her drive for success.

But with her conjunction here all together the Sun, Jupiter and ambitious North Node, she was here to be her! You don't remember her significant relationships as much as the photos of herself solo in famous photographs smiling.

She had vigor from these Aries planets. Her Mars, however, in Cancer in the 6th house of health, was in a weak placement so here we see her history of a frail constitution.

Her shining Piscean qualities were embedded in her super electric and compassionate combo of Venus in Pisces conjunct Uranus. This made her attractive and magnetic to be around.

Her Aquarius rising made her a humanitarian, champion for human rights.

The moon on the rise made her quite an empath and very sensitive.

Her Saturn in Sagittarius gave her the drive to settle only for the truth.

"Nothing is impossible, the word itself say's 'I'm possible'!"

"For beautiful eyes, look for the good in others; for beautiful lips, speak only words of kindness; and for poise, walk with the knowledge that you are never alone."

"As you grow older, you will discover that you have two hands, one for helping yourself, the other for helping others."

"People, even more than things, have to be restored, renewed, revived, reclaimed, and redeemed; never throw out anyone."

Taurus

May 15 - June 14

Ruled by Venus
Element: Earth
Color: White
Gemstone: Diamond
Body: the Throat

Taurus is a sign that is sensitive to the beautiful things in life. Ruled by the relationship planet Venus, they are lovers and enjoy the finer things in life. Sensual and artistic they enjoy the pleasures of this world. The tactile value of earthly things are apparent to the Taurus. They are often seen wearing designer bags and clothing, diamonds, and are smart about investments. They buy beautiful things of lasting value. Relationships, arts, music, and fine dining, all hold a special place to the Taurus.

They can find themselves working in the beauty industry, arts, music, culinary field or in finances. They usually have an earthy beauty of their own. They are slow to act. Venus influence makes keeps them from being impulsive, they take their time and enjoy themselves. This energy can bring a steady mind and heart. Taureans take enjoyment in simple pleasures and just being.

If you thought you were a Gemini and now find yourself as a Taurus, try to reconsider. As a true Taurus, you may resist or be slow to adapt to this new perspective. You may find you want things more solid and status quo. Your approach is not one of a risk taker.

Taurus is ruled by Venus. If Venus falls in Taurus it is very strong for finances, love and money.

The moon is exalted in its favorite sign of Taurus, with contentment and inner peace is the side effect.

Taurus Sun People:

Janet Jackson - May 16
Megan Fox - May 16
Tina Fey - May 18
Cher - May 20
Bob Dylan May 24
Lenny Kravitz - May 26
John F. Kennedy - May 29
Krishna Das - May 31
Clint Eastwood - May 31
Morgan Freeman - June 1
Alanis Morisette June 1
Marilyn Monroe - June 1
Angelina Jolie - June 4
Bar Raphael - June 4
Prince - June 7
Johnny Depp - June 9
Shia Le Beouf - June 11
Hugh Laurie - June 11
Donald Trump - June 14

Taurus Chart Study

Angelina Jolie
6/4/1975
Los Angeles, CA
9:09am

Rising Sign: Cancer
Sun Sign: Taurus
Moon Sign: Pisces

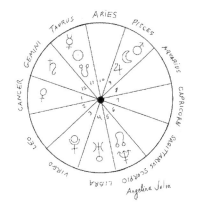

Angelina Jolie

At first glance Angelina's chart reveals a Venus in Cancer on the rise. We see her caring for children and the world, and with Venus' help, a beauty that will shine thru her whole life.

Her Sun is in Tropical Gemini, but in Sidereal it is in Taurus, showing her solid yet sensual demeanor. Taurus lends a stability, devotion and cool. Its ruler, Venus like to takes its time as it is enjoying all the beauty life has. They are slow to act as they are involved in the material nature of things.

Mercury is nearby her Sun, also in the later degrees of Taurus. This is in a star cluster shared with the early degrees of Gemini, so here we see what looks like a "Gemini Sun." Here she shows bright ideas and a voice to speak up, yet she remains quiet about much with the South Node nearby. On the other side of her Sun is the South Node. When this is with the Sun sign it can bring up challenges like rejection, separation or some loss about the father figure. It is a pastille influence and this is a classic combination for relationship issues with the father.

Her strong feelings of compassion and her spirituality and wisdom comes through with her three planets in Pisces. Jupiter and the Moon brings feelings of well being, and Mars in any planetary combination can bring conflict. This could explain her roles in high action films. It is also in opposition Pluto, showing some control issues, drama and intrigue for the macabre can come to the surface.

Her Cancer rising sign shows her need to be a caretaker and protector for the children and world causes.

"Without pain, there would be no suffering. Without suffering, we would never learn from our mistakes. To make it right, pain and suffering is the key to all windows, without it, there is no way of life."

"When I get logical, and I don't trust my instincts - that's when I get in trouble."

Gemini

June 15 - July 16

Ruled by Mercury
Element of Air
Color: Green
Gem : Emerald
Body: The Mind

Light and airy, a conversation comes easy with the Gemini. Our friends, eternally in relationship, are quick thinking with a twinkle in the eye. You will find them at their best in the neighborhood and the casual happenings of everyday life. They may spend time on the internet, blogging, and on the phone sharing information and ideas with others. Gemini's people are news and information junkies with a lot of chit chat to share.

They may be constantly learning about new things for work, and can be the master sales person, able to outsell others with quick thinking, facts and witty replies.

Emotions can run on the surface, and you might not know where they are at, until one day their changeable nature surprises you. Changing things up is a lifestyle for them!

They can thrive in offices. They are able to juggle phone calls, paper work and personal relationship skills all at once. They often are lean and lanky, nervous, living as it were, on air.

If you thought you were a Cancer, you may be relieved to acknowledge your clear thinking, logical, mercurial intelligence.

Cancers ruled by the moon are intuitive, caretakers and family oriented bosses. You may be more of an adventurer who enjoys changing things up and getting out and about than a controlling leader who wants things a certain way.

The planet Mercury placed in Gemini is its full strength, masculine ruler and brings a super clear intellect and a logical thinker. Mercury in Virgo is its feminine counterpart and it also brings intelligence.

Gemini Sun People:

Courtney Cox - June 15
Tupac - June 16
Nicole Kidman - June 20
Meryl Streep - June 22
George Michael - June 25
Michael Phelps - June 30
Pamela Andersen - July 1
Princess Diana - July 1
Liv Tyler - July 1
Lindsey Lohan - July 2
Tom Cruise - July 3
Frida Khalo - July 6
HH the Dalai Lama - July 6
George W. Bush - July 6
Sylvester Stallone - July 6
50 Cent - July 6
Tom Hanks - July 9
Sophia Vergara July 10
Jessica Simpson - July 10
Harrison Ford - July 13

Gemini Chart Study:

HH the Dalai Lama
7/6/1935
Tengster Village, Tibet
4:38am

Rising Sign: Gemini
Sun Sign: Gemini
Moon Sign: Leo

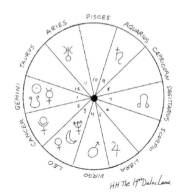

HH The 14th Dalai Lama

His Holiness The Dalai Lama really shows his Gemini influence in the way he meets and greets people all around the global neighborhood. Though he is considered a Cancer in Tropical zodiac, it is easy to see the mercurial qualities of his rising sign and Sun sign in Gemini. He is easy going with conversation and friendliness. He brings much information, wisdom teachings and commonsense to the world.

With his rising sign, Mercury and Sun all conjunct in Gemini, he greets us all. But with the South Node also there, a spiritualization happens in this first house of self and we find someone very giving and genuinely more interested in others than himself.

His Venus, Moon and Neptune conjunct in Leo gives him a loving and pleasant disposition, and high vibration energies. This is in the third house of communications, ruled by Gemini so we continue with the mercurial influence.

This combination of planets brings a compassionate and playful nature. Communications with others is key to his chart. This creativity is influenced by Neptune, which brings him awareness to the higher frequencies and realms.

His Cancer influence involves Pluto, in the second house of Cancer, and also Mars in the second house of home, family and Mother. Here you can see these planets had their dramatic influences on his home and family life. He was taken from his family to be a young king, and of course the loss of his country with its aggressive take over from China.

"Be kind whenever possible. It is always possible."

"My religion is very simple. My religion is kindness."

"This is my simple religion. There is no need for temples; no need for complicated philosophy. Our own brain, our own heart is our temple; the philosophy is kindness." "Love and compassion are necessities, not luxuries. Without them, humanity cannot survive."

Cancer

July 17 - August 16

Ruled by the Moon
Element of Water
Color: White
Gem: Pearl/Moonstone
Body: the Chest

I know, you seem so loving and caring and family oriented...and Leo seem like an apt poetic description, but unlike Leo, you are ruled by the Moon, and water. That Leo quality you apply is really Cancer's supportive loving and nurturing moon energy.

The Moon in it's ruling sign says all about why you care about so many people. It also attracts many people to you. If you are a man, women can feel drawn to you because you hold the lunar energy they can identify and you can serve them with. If you are a woman, the Moon and water energy can magnify your womanly and maternal energy. You may become the big brother and big sister to your friends, head of household and company. Both sexes can become cosmic caretakers and family planners, and though they hold dynamic energy, they also wish to be reciprocated with loving and caring.

This is a creative sign, a controlling sign, and a very intuitive sign. Emotions are the fuel you run on and you keep yourself in your protective shell, figuratively and literally. You may not feel right unless you have a nice car and home adding a feeling of security. This water sign is a crab, with a shell to protect its vulnerable insides. Because of all this sensitivity, and crabby feelers, you may try to control things and become very demonstrative about having it your way. They are the classic zodiac enabler, they see what needs to be done and can do too much for others.

One way to note the difference is wardrobes: The Cancer will behave sensitively, dress in a calming, soothing folk singer-like manner, and the Leo will probably have some real out going wardrobe items, lion mane-like hairdos, and dramatic personalities.

Planets best to have in Cancer: the Moon and Jupiter. When the moon or Jupiter are in Cancer, we get feelings of wholeness, healing and contentment.

Cancer Sun People:

Vin Diesel - July 18
Richard Branson - July 18
Benedict Cumberbatch - July 19
Gisele Bündchen - July 20
Ernest Hemingway - July 21
Daniel Radcliffe - July 23
Jennifer Lopez - July 24
Mic Jagger - July 26
Jackie Kennedy-Onassis - July 28
Arnold Schwarzenegger - July 30
JK Rowling - July 31
Barack Obama - August 4
Andy Warhol - August 6
Whiney Houston - August 9
Antonio Banderas - August 10
Cara Delevingne - Aug 12
Halle Berry - August 14
Mila Kunis - August 14
Madonna - August 16

Cancer Chart Study:

Mic Jagger
July 24, 1942
Dartford UK
2:30am

Rising Sign: Taurus
Sun Sign: Cancer
Moon Sign: Taurus

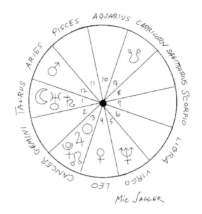

Mic Jagger

Mic Jagger is the well known singer from the Rolling Stones. His Sun sign in Tropical is Leo, but in Sidereal it actually falls in Cancer. It is in the company of Jupiter, the North Node and Pluto, all in Cancer. This adds worldly power and fortune to the moon ruled sign of Cancer, accentuating it in these different planets. He has 8 kids and 5 baby Mommas, and grandchildren. Cancer males are ultimate love magnets for women as well.

I have found that the generic astrological information about Leo is often a created image that is "Mic Jaggerish." It is a very classic misdiagnosis the cancer person being a leo. A charismatic rockstar who runs about singing with what looks like no inhibition. However, it is worth a second look. Even the way he moves back and forth on stage is rather crab like movements.

When we look more closely we do see Venus is placed in Leo. This brings in a dose of creativity and romance. But here it in his fourth house which is influenced as the Cancer ruled house. Venus placed here also shows special talents in the arts and a big heart.

His rising sign is in Taurus, a Venus ruled sign. Relationships, music, and money and his unique vocals are important influencers in his chart. He also has three planets on the rise. With the moon on the rise, he has great sensitivity, and Uranus brings independence, rebelliousness, and add Saturnine seriousness. This allowed him to use his gifts, applying discipline that Saturn brings to ground and grow through time.

Lose your dreams and you might lose your mind.

Anything worth doing is worth overdoing.

It's all right letting yourself go, as long as you can get yourself back.

Anarchy is the only slight glimmer of hope.

Leo

August 17 - September 16

Ruled by the Sun
Element of Fire
Color: Burgundy
Gem: Ruby
Body : The Heart

Leo is a sign ruled by the Sun, the largest heavenly body in our solar system. The purity and energy of the Sun is a magical, mystical wonderful thing. Leo carries this strong clear aura of the Sun. A brightness shines from with in that warms people up.

There is a regal quality about the stature Leo. You, of all the zodiac, can truly be yourself. Filled with personality and creativity, Leo's like to laugh and enjoy themselves, people, kids and parties. They are frequently entertainers, artists and business people and bring a warmth with their smile. They enjoy the company of children, and can be found kidding around.

Leo can carry authority and be leaders in their field. They rule their own kingdoms, and often can be seen multitasking and organizing in other peoples worlds.

Like a cat, one minute they are purring and the next they withdraw that sunshine and are alone up in the tree. The biggest surprise is when you find out your warm sunny friend needs a little alone time.

Very often the complaints that can be surrounding Leo, such as "oh I can't stand Leos!" are misdirected. These complaints belong back a sign...in Cancer! So when you go complaining about Leo, just remember if was probably one of those sensitive, controlling Moon people! Meanwhile the true Leo is trying to be a big kitty, fitting into a Virgo cereal box.

In Indian astrology the Sun is a chariot driver, with twelve Horses pulling his reigns, as compared to Tropical zodiac assignment of the Virgo woman of purity.

The Planet you want in Leo: The Sun. The sun is ruled by Leo, so here is the pure soul of the self represented by the sun.

Leo Sun People:

Sean Penn - August 17
Robert De Niro - August 17
Robert Redford - August 18
Bill Clinton - August 19
Coco Chanel - August 19
Gene Roddenberry - August 19
Demi Lovato - Aug 20
Robert Plant - August 20
Sean Connery - August 25
Tim Burton - August 25
Mother Teresa - August 26
Michael Jackson - August 29
Cameron Diaz-August 30
Richard Gere - August 31
Barry Gibb - Sept 1
Dr. Phil - Sept 1
Salma Hayek - Sept 2
Charlie Sheen - September 3
Beyonce - Sept 4
Freddie Mercury - September 5
Adam Sandler - Sept 9
Amy Winehouse - Sept 14
Mickey Rourke - Sept 16

Leo Chart Study

Freddie Mercury
September 5 1946
6:30am
Zanzibar, Tanzania.

Rising Sign: Leo
Sun Sign: Leo
Moon Sign : Sagittarius

This Leo who is considered a Virgo in Tropical astrology, this lead singer, vocalist, song writer, and record producer radiated charisma and the pure expression of the heart. He dubbed himself 'Freddie Mercury'.

The sun in Leo is in its own sign, and in Freddie's case it's magnified by being on the rise in its ruling sign. This gave him a double Leo status and brought much power and magnetism. Add to it Mercury also on the rise in Leo, and you have someone that becomes the mouthpiece for communication coming straight from the heart of the Lion. The first house, as mentioned in the houses section earlier in the book, is all about manifesting the self and having to be true to oneself. And Leo is the pure expression of the self.

As we look at his second house, this is the house of the voice. Here he has his Mars in Virgo. This Mars, with nearby Neptune gave him a mystical dimension to his voice, expressed easily and with the skill and craftsmanship that Virgo in this degree can bestow.

Third house strength is communications and willpower. Here he had Venus in Libra, with much strength in its own sign. It is conjunct Jupiter showing flair for relationships, art, music, socializing, parties and great advice and artistic insight. Jupiter just magnified it all the more and he really had that kind of life.

His home life was never really comfortable to him. He was far more headed towards fame and public life and with Rahu, the shadowy north node, Uranus in his tenth it made him famously infamous for being unconventional.

What we didn't see is his ability to be very powerful from behind he scenes. Like a great general, his Saturn and Pluto in the 12th house of retreat helped him to think, plan and meditate things from behind the scenes. I think it also made him feel a helpless loneliness. This influence was connected to his creative 5th house moon, in Sagittarius. This helped him convey the suffering the 12th house could bring and express it. The moon in first degrees of Sagittarius, showed an optimistic and philosophical disposition. And an ability to cut off if hurt.

"The reason we're successful, darling? My overall charisma, of course."

"I was born to love you with every single beat of my heart. I was born to take care of you every single day of your life."

Virgo

September 17 - October 16
Ruled by Mercury
Element: earth
Color: Green
Gemstone: Emerald
Body: Stomach/Digestion

To become a Virgo is not a demotion from Libra status. "what, no, I'm a Libra!" But if you knew having natural beauty, smarts and two feet on the ground is a Virgos upside, then you might not mind. You are practical (earth) and intelligent (mercury) and hold space for simplicity.

Most people would rather be considered a lovely Libra, not a generically watered down fussy Virgo. But I don't see it that way. Having your Sun in Virgo makes for a smart, discerning, solid person. Please enjoy the description: intelligent, intellectual, refined, even with a flare for craftsmanship in the arts. A sensual beauty that comes from the simplicity that only an earth sign can have. There is a slight inwardness and reserve here, which... well that makes them more alluring.

Your approach to grooming and clothing is way more refined in a simple way than Venus ruled Libra. In fact, this is a great way to understand your a Virgo. Heavy make up and flashy designer clothes are not your choice in appearances. You may also find health and fitness to be your best beauty treatment. Diet and the commonsense of care taking oneself is natural to a Virgo.

Your ruler, Mercury, is inward turned here bringing humility and modesty. Serving and helping others is more satisfying than being in the spot light for Virgo.

Virgos are very discerning. Just as they digestive tract is the area of the body ruled by Virgo, they have a natural sense of order. They can break things down and organize.

Communications and service are also Virgo traits. You know they love you if they do you a favor, clean or provide some kind of service.

The best planet to have in Virgo is Mercury. It is exalted here and promotes clear thinking and the love of study.

Virgo Sun People:

Greta Garbo - Sept 18
Jimmy Fallon - September 19
Sophia Loren - Sept 20
Steven King - Sept 21
Leonard Cohen - Sept 21
Will Smith - September 25
Catherine Zeta-Jones - Sept 25
Heather Locklear - Sept 25
Ray Charles - Sept 23
Bruce Springsteen - Sept 23
Gwenyth Paltrow - Sept 27
Bridget Bardo - September 28
Mahatma Gandhi - October 2
Sting - October 2
Gwen Stefani - October 3
Susan Sarandon - October 4
Ray Kroc - September 4
Kate Winslet - October 5
Vladimir Putin - October 7
John Lennon - October 9
Luciano Pavarotti - Oct 12
Hugh Jackman - October 12
Usher - October 14
Oscar Wilde - October 1

Virgo Chart Study:

John Lennon
10/9/1940
6:30PM
Liverpool England

Rising Sign: Pisces
Sun Sign: Virgo
Moon Sign: Capricorn

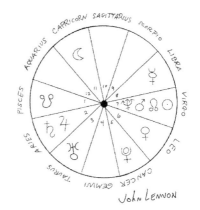

John LENNON

John Lennon is not a Libra as in Tropical Zodiac. His mild mannered and reserved Virgo Sun in Sidereal time resides in the 7th house that rules relationships. This adds a Libra like influence. His sun is also in a stellium, with the worldly North Node, and nearby is Mars softened by its conjunction with Neptune.

His rising sign, or first house is in Pisces, with the South node. So what we first see with John is his spiritual Pisces influence, very self sacrificing, taking emphasis off himself and putting it into relationships. Relationships were his way to grow. He was known as a singer and song writer. His mercury ruled Virgo planets gave him his best skill with writing and singing the song, rather than actual musicianship.

John Lennon is remembered as being part of relationships or another way to explain it he worked well in collaborations. An example of this is his Lennon/McCartney duo for song writing, his partnership with the Beatles. The Beatles dissolved and he focused on his work with Yoko. It is that we remember him with these other important players in his life shows this strong influence from his relationship house and self sacrificing first house. But this is not a Sun in Libra.

His Mercury was is in Libra, in the 8th house. He was a deep thinker, and needed to share this communication to others was his Libra influence. He thought in peace and balance.
His Saturn conjunct Jupiter shows his deeply spiritual ascetic nature.

"All we are saying is give peace a chance."

"Imagine all the people living life in peace. You may say I'm a dreamer, but I'm not the only one. I hope someday you'll join us, and the world will be as one."

"A dream you dream alone is only a dream. A dream you dream together is reality."

"Time you enjoy wasting, was not wasted."

"Reality leaves a lot to the imagination."

Libra

October 17 - November 15
Ruled by Venus
Element: Air
Color: White
Gemstone: Diamond
Body: Kidney

Well, now that you found out you're really a Libra, consider it to be one of the top desirable signs! "No, Im a Scorpio…!" Sorry, but all that sleek sexiness you exude is due to the planet Venus. That attractive vibe of beauty and pizazz arrives thru the gift of Venus. And all those partners and relationships you crave and cannot live without, are due to the relationship oriented powers Venus brings. You are the original romantics. You put the "co" into codependent.

With the Sun is in Libra there is, however, a little glitch. Your ego, represented by the SUN, is our pure sense of self. Here the Sun takes a fall. In Libra the Sun becomes a Venus ruled sign. The Libran takes their own identity thru the partnerships with others. They depend on others. They are the most married sign of the Zodiac. They often are discussing their partners or relationship issues, or are seen hanging with their friends. They are influenced by what their friends do. The self wants to share here, it wants relationships. It learns from and relies on the other. Libra needs the reflection of others to find themselves. Venus brings in the charm, artistic flare, social graces, love of company and good times.

I think this is why it is so important for them to be identified as a

Scorpio. Because the generic idea that scorpio attracts so many partners with their charms and sex appeal. But really, this is exactly what they need to watch out for, that they do not lose themselves for the other. They do have musical and artistic taste and talent, a sense of balance, line and color. They like flowers, fine dining and peaceful environments. They understand the value in beautiful things like diamonds and luxury items. Dressing beautifully and grooming is important to them. They can be a little lazy and indulgent, as Venus enjoys the pleasures and doesn't want to get its hands dirty. Consider its opposite, Aries: active, direct and independent.

Some planets are strong in Libra. The planets you want in Libra: Venus and Saturn.

Libra Sun People:

Eminem - October 17
Zac Effron - October 18
Silvia Brown - October 19
Snoop Dogg - October 20
Kim Kardashian - Oct 21
Carrie Fisher - Oct 21
Catherine Deneuve - Oct 22
Depak Chopra - Oct 22
Ryan Reynolds - October 23
Katy Perry - Oct 25
Pablo Picasso - Oct 25
Hillary Clinton - October 26
Keith Urban - October 26
Julia Roberts - October 28
Caitlin (Bruce) Jenner - October 28
Bill Gates - October 28
Aishwarya Rai - November 1
Marie Antoinette - November 2
Matthew McConaughey - Nov 4
Ethan Hawke - Nov 6
Richard Burton - November 10
Leonardo DiCaprio - November 11
Demi Moore - November 11
Grace Kelly - November 12
Whoopi Goldberg - November 13
Prince Charles - November 14

Libra Chart Study

Leonardo DiCaprio
11/11/1974
2:47am
Los Angeles, California

Rising Sign: Virgo
Sun Sign: Libra
Moon Sign: Virgo

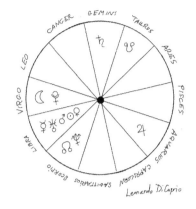

Leonardo DiCaprio

As we unfold the Sidereal zodiac story, we find a well dressed, and fair featured, Libra man, who is misdiagnosed as a Scorpio. He has a focused stellium in Libra. Venus, Sun, Mars, Mercury and Uranus line up in Libra. His ordinarily "debilitated" Sun in Libra gains a lot of support. These planets all reside in the solid second house. Planets here can give people powers of stability and speech. His strongly placed Venus in its own sign conjunct the Sun brings its artistic talents. Mars brings energy and drive. Uranus and Mercury bring genius and forward thinking. Just sugar coat all this with the icing of Libra charm. He has had several long term relationships with some of the most beautiful models in the world. Venus is so tight to the sun, however, it is burnt out, and he may feel under appreciated, seen in how he though nominated, he went 23 years without actually winning an academy award.

His moon is on the rise in Virgo, in the first house of self. Virgo is the digestive system itself and he is known to lean towards a vegan diet. The moon gives him sensitivity and emotional appeal, and bringing with it the classic inward nature of reserved Virgo. Pluto on the rise with his moon brings in power, and all kinds of sizzling intensity. Add to it the mercurial influence of Saturn in Gemini in the 10th house of career and you have a very responsible man with communication being a key in his career and public life. He started the Leonardo DiCaprio Foundation, an environmental group and backed the movie Cowspiracy, an environmental film about the impact of animal agriculture on the environment. His Jupiter in the 6th house in Aquarius brings him many helpful friends and desire to help humanitarian causes. He is a sprinkled with so mch mercurial influences he is a great spokesman.

So as for Scorpio, it rules his 3rd house, which again can show literary talent, writing, communications. The north node placed here guides him towards growth in this life towards Scorpio, developing depth, sensitivity in speech and transformation.

> "Raising awareness on the most pressing environmental issues of our time is more important than ever."

> "To believe in love, to be ready to give up anything for it, to be willing to risk your life for it, is the ultimate tragedy."

> "I get a friend to travel with me... I need somebody to bring me back to who I am. It's hard to be alone."

Scorpio

November 16 - December 15
Ruled by Mars
Element: Water
Color: Red
Gemstone: Red Coral
Body: Reproduction organs

Here we see the transformational energies of a Scorpio misunderstood as an optimistic truth seeker known as Sagittarius. By contrast, an inward nature is easy to see in our secretive Scorpio friends. Intuition and feeling are a Scorpios way of working. These sensitive folks operate from the heart chakra to that root chakra and don't miss a trick. Like deep wizards of healing and insight, they have been living with their own personal challenges and are adept at grasping the deeper issues of life.

All that passion, focus and direction is brought to you from the ruling planet of Mars. Here it is simmering in deep dark waters. Feelings are in the quiet depths. With much transformational and challenging energies to handle, you become used to the ride. You are protective and powerful. A loyal friend and vengeful enemy is found here. The higher vibration Scorpio is intuitive as water, and applies their energy for helping heal others.

Often they will feel more well balanced when applying some kind of physical exercise routine, like the gym, tennis, martial arts or yoga. Scorpios actually enjoy and add fitness to their life. There are the more introverted ones whose steam never quite gets expressed, but they have a life-force reserve of energy. This is also why there is so much popular reference to their "sexiness." Here the sexual-emotional nature expresses life force.

Mars is not a fancy ruling sign, so they do not need too much adornment, they stick to simplicity. Sometimes the athletic look suits them the best. They are generally fond of blending in to environments. This sign is more interested in seeing thru to who you are than what you look like. This is a big clue for the sidereal Libra that you are not a Scorpio.

Mars is in Scorpio it very strong, bringing health, vitality, stamina and motivation.

Scorpio Sun People:

Martin Scorsese - November 17
Steven Spielberg - December 18
Bjork - November 21
Goldie Hawn - November 21
Scarlett Johansson - November 22
Sathya Sai Baba - November 23
Miley Cyrus - November 23
Ted Bundy - November 24
Bruce Lee November 27
Jimi Hendrix - November 27
Anna Nicole Smith - November 28
Woody Allen - December 1
Brittany Spears - December 2
Nelly Furtado - December 2
Julianne Moore - December 3
Jay Z - December 4
Tyra Banks - December 4
Sinead O'Connor - December 8
Jim Morrison - December 8
Nicky Minaj - December 8
Kim Bassinger - December 8
Osho - December 11
Frank Sinatra - Dec 12
Taylor Swift - December 13
Vanessa Hudgens - December 14
Nostradamus - December 14

Scorpio Chart Study:

December 2, 1981
1:30am
Mc Comb MS

Rising Sign: Virgo
Sun Sign: Scorpio
Moon Sign: Capricorn

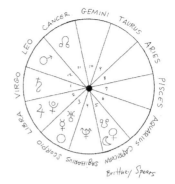

Brittney Spears

Brittany is a classic case of a misdiagnosed Sagittarius.

Here in Sidereal Zodiac she is a Scorpio.

Does this make any sense to y'all? Also nearby her Sun in scorpio is in a radical and rebellious conjunction with Uranus. She also has a nearby Mercury gifting her with communication skills. So here she is, a passionate, outspoken innovator. With her Scorpio Sun she has deep sensitivity, sensuality and vibes.

She also has Saturn in Virgo on the rise, which in many cases shows responsibility from a very early age in life. She can actually be able to handle a lot of pressure, and carry out the work and deal with the karma. In performance though, it shows she brings some reserve to the stage.

She is one of these beauties with Virgo as the rising sign, giving her that natural beauty only Virgo can bestow. So her Scorpio nature gets a filter. She is one of those Stars that is in basic Starbucks coffee shots and is seen in her everyday glory. Her famous outfits are not far from fitness clothing gone glam.

Her fifth house Moon/Venus conjunction bestows her charm and friendliness. The Moon/Ketu combination shows a special relationship with her Mom, and gives her heightened sensitivity and intuition. The Venus/ketu combination can show she has challenges in relationships and may not get the satisfaction from close personal relationships. This life she needs to focus more on the outer life and the public.

"I don't like defining myself. I just am."

"With love, you should go ahead and take the risk of getting hurt... because love is an amazing feeling."

"Onstage I'm the happiest person in the world."

"Sundance is weird. The movies are weird - you actually have to think about them when you watch them."

"Just because I look sexy on the cover of Rolling Stone doesn't mean I'm naughty.

"I know not everyone will like me, but this is who I am so if you don't like it, tough!"

Sagittarius

December 16 - January 14

Ruled by Jupiter
Element: Fire
Color: Yellow
Gemstone: Yellow Sapphire
Body: Hips

Many people with this placement as a sidereal Capricorn told me they never felt like they were a Capricorn. A Sagittarian is just like that: they can sense and know the truth. This is a gift of the ruling planet Jupiter. Jupiter brings this wisdom, optimism and energy to go with it.

A true Sun in Sagittarius has evolved from the depths of Scorpio and thru those lessons has climbed to a new plateau. The Sun is strong when its in Sagittarius, and they have self confidence and enthusiasm. Travel and adventure is their favorite past time. Here you find the optimist, the exhibitionist, the philosopher, people involved in law and higher learning. They are fond of world religions and are natural students of life.

They have a good sense of themselves and have the natural independence of a fire sign and the bonus blessings of Jupiter. They are natural teachers about the deeper meaning of life where wisdom is the wellspring.

The Sagittarius can be straight forward about delivering you just what they think. Diplomacy and tact can take a backseat to the truth here.

It is tough to have been misdiagnosed as a Capricorn, with the constrictive rings of Saturn. "Don't fence me in" is more like their theme song. You are really the archer, a golden child of Jupiter.

Wardrobes include colors and multicultural themes. T-shirts with meaning and music groups are ok with them. They might even be found wearing hippy beads and crystals.

Jupiter is strong when placed in Sagittarius. This further magnifies the need for truth and exploration, and a person who is good with advice.

Sagittarius Sun People

Ludwig Van Beethoven - Dec 16
Pope Francis - Dec 17
Paul Klee - December 18
Brat Bitt - December 18
Katie Holmes - December 18
Keith Richards - December 18
Jane Fonda - December 21
Vanessa Paradis - Dec 22
Ricky Martin - December 24
Annie Lenox - December 25
Gerard Depardieu - December 27
Tiger Woods - December 30
Anthony Hopkins - Dec 31
Christy Turlington - January 2
Mel Gibson - January 3
Isaac Newton - January 4
Brad Cooper - January 5
January Jones - January 5
Joan of Arc - January 6
Nicolas Cage - January 7-
David Bowie - January 8
Elvis - January 8
Jimmy Page - January 9
Joan Baez - January 9
Swami Vivekananda - January 12
Liam Hemsworth - January 13

Sagittarius Chart Study

January 8, 1947
9:00am
Brixton, London

Rising Sign: Capricorn
Sun Sign: Sagittarius
Moon Sign: Cancer

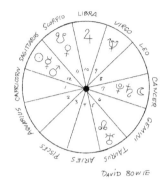

David Bowie is a great example of someone who is born a Sidereal Time Sagittarius. We do see an influence from Capricorn in his rising sign, this influence can easily be seen in his no-nonsense demeanor. His tropical zodiac Sun was Capricorn, so here is the case that his Sun is Sagittarius, but other influences, such as the rising sign is in Capricorn. So he had both qualities.

He was confident with a good sense of himself. He was a far out truth seeker. Sagittarius is in love with truth and philosophy. His Sagittarius Sun, Mars and Mercury all line up in the spiritual vibrations of the 12th house, bringing this high vibration spirituality to his work. This is where he needed some quiet solitude in his life.

He had Saturn, Pluto and Moon all in his relationship house so he was not alone. In his song, 'Lets Dance' the line invites his partner to dance in the serious moonlight. This song captures the essence of the moon/pluto/saturn in his seventh house. Saturn conjunct his moon with Pluto... we had some Very serious intense Moonlight from Mr. Bowie! He had a lot of responsibility for others, caused by these planets in his relationship house. He also found emotional fulfillment with the moons presence here. And in seventh house fashion he also married a famous partner, the international model, Iman.

Jupiter in Libra in his 10th career house shows work in the arts and Venus in Scorpio in his 11th public pressures house shows his artistic nature, and his gift of sharing himself with others. Uranus and the north node in Taurus lent fame for innovations and radical futuristic vision.

"Tomorrow belongs to those who can hear it coming"

"Don't let me hear you say life takes you nowhere, angel"

"If it works, it's out of date"

"Ive always had a repulsive need to be something more than human"

"Religion is for people who fear hell, spirituality is for people that have been there"

Capricorn

January 15 - February 13

ruled by Saturn
Element: Earth
Color: Black
Gemstone: Blue Sapphire
Body: Knees

A traditional sign like Capricorn, confused as a quirky Aquarian? Perhaps you never quite felt the Aquarian thing fit, but you accepted it per tradition. Capricorn is a reserved sign that has a level head. Even in childhood the Capricorn child seems mature ahead of their time. There is an inward nature to the Capricorn.

They are more oriented to the basics and bare bones of things, to thrift and practicality. Though there is a melancholic disposition, it comes with insight and a deadpan sense of humor.

There is a certain inner quietness and reserve to the personality. They can carry tradition, and be it conservative, or hardcore, they will walk the talk of their chosen tradition.

They are loyal, and with Saturn as the ruling planet, there is sensitivity, an etheric nature. This is not an emotional sign. They can take on leadership roles and be very strong. They often can carry a lot of responsibility. They are of a serious nature and are able to exert self control. They often found as administrators and can handle big business. They can carry the work load, and are the supervisor to their peers.

When the planet Saturn is in Capricorn, it is at its best, and able to handle the pressures of Saturn with ease. He becomes the commander here.

The planet Mars in Capricorn is very strong and committed to work for the cause and becomes the general in this placement.

Capricorn Sun People:

Martin Luther King - January 15
Kate Moss - January 16
Jim Carrey - January 17
Michelle Obama - January 17
Mohammed Ali - January 17
Cary Grant - January 18
Al Capone - January 18
Janis Joplin - January 19
Edgar Allen Poe - January 19
Alicia Keys - January 25
Paul Newman - January 26
Ellen DeGeneres - January 26
Wolfgang Amadeus Mozart - January 27
Oprah Winfrey - January 29
Christian Bale - January 30
Justin Timberlake - January 31
Harry Styles - February 1
Shakira - February 2
Christie Brinkley - February 2
Amal Clooney - February 3
Rosa Parks - February 4
Bob Marley - February 6
Axl Rose - February 6
Ashton Kutcher - February 7
James Dean - February 8
Taylor Lautner - February 11
Jennifer Anniston - February 11
Abraham Lincoln - February 12
Christina Ricci - February 12

Capricorn Chart Study:

1/25/1958
3:00am
Metaire LA

Rising Sign: Scorpio
Sun Sign: Capricorn
Moon Sign: Pisces

Ellen Degeneres

Ellen was considered an Aquarian in Tropical zodiac but here we see she is a Sidereal Capricorn. Her hard working commitment to show biz and even sense of humor can be seen with a Capricorn Sun. We have to note, it is conjunct Venus. This Venus influence gives her a more graceful manner, friendliness and makes her a relationship person. It extends her charm and sociability. Capricorns by nature are a little melancholy but Venus will lighten it. She's sensitive and very compassionate with the Moon in Pisces.

When we consider her rising sign, we see her strength as Saturn is on the rise in Scorpio. Ellen has been responsible from a young age, and knows how to carry a lot of responsibility.

Her stellium in Libra includes Jupiter, Neptune and The North Node. This shows a very high vibe. It also shows she needs to go towards relationships in this life. It is filled with natural wisdom and a drive for success.

Her Saturn is very close to Mars giving her great powers as the commander and the general. So we see a leader with a sense of humor and kindness in Ellens chart. She has no planets or influence from her Tropical Zodiac diagnosis as an Aquarius to note.

"Procrastinate now, don't put it off."

"I really don't think I need buns of steel. I'd be happy with buns of cinnamon."

129

"People always ask me, 'Were you funny as a child?' Well, no, I was an accountant."

"In the beginning there was nothing. God said, 'Let there be light!' And there was light. There was still nothing, but you could see it a whole lot better."

"I was raised around heterosexuals, as all heterosexuals are, that's where us gay people come from... you heterosexuals."

Aquarius

February 13 - March 14

Ruled by Saturn{traditional}
Element : Air
Color: Black
Gemstone: Blue Sapphire
Body: Ankles

Now I know, you wanted to be that mystical Pisces, but friend, it's gonna be okay. An Aquarian is an advanced zodiac member like the Piscean, but you have more detachment (air) and have a calling to practical matters, service and responsibilities (Saturn). Aquarius is depicted as the water bearer, not because of the watery nature of emotions, but because of his giving and service. This is a more structured energy than what our fishy friends have to deal with. But don't fear. You will find qualities of deep universal understanding are there.

Aquarius is evolved in the zodiac journey. They are more attuned with reality more than day dreaming. They are socially conscious. They are concerned more with serving humanity, then ruling the Kingdom. Caring for society, and seeing the big picture is Aquarius forte. There is an energy that can enjoy groups and being in the social arena, yet they can be very private, reserved and aloof. The practical, conserved and hardworking side blends with the idealism of Air.

They can be found in a team, a group of friends, at music events, spiritual groups, with groups of work friends, and enjoying being a part of social outings. They can be medicine workers and doctors, nurses, teachers.

The planet Saturn is strong in Aquarius as it gives a good work ethic, drive for focus and responsibility.

Aquarius Sun People:

Eckhart Tolle - February 16
Ed Sheeran - February 17
Paris Hilton - February 17
Michael Jordan - February 17
Denise Richards - February 17
John Travolta - February 18
Dr. Dre - February 18
Yoko Ono - February 18
Rhianna - February 20
Kurt Cobain - February 20
Cindy Crawford - February 20
Alan Rickman - February 21
Jennifer Love Hewitt - February 21
Dakota Fanning - February 23
Steve Jobs - February 24
George Harrison - February 24
Johnny Cash - February 26
Elizabeth Taylor - February 27
Tony Robbins - February 29
Justin Bieber - March 1
Frederic Chopin - March 1
Kesha - March 1
Jon Bon Jovi - March 2
Michelangelo - March 6
Shaquille O'Neal - March 6
Sharon Stone - March 10
Olivia Wilde - March 10
John Hamm - March 10
Jack Kerouac - March 12
Liza Minelli - March 12
Albert Einstein - March 14

AQUARIUS Chart Study:

LIZ TAYLOR
FEBRUARY 23, 1932
2:30am
Hampstead, UK

Rising Sign: Scorpio
Sun Sign: Aquarius
Moon sign: Libra

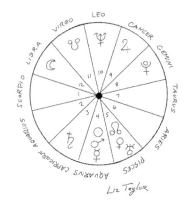

Liz Taylor is considered a Pisces in Western Astrology, but in Sidereal time her Sun sign is Aquarius. Her Mercury and Mars are also in Aquarius conjunct the Sun. Mercury here gave her some skills at communication, but also mental strain. Her Mars in this tight conjunction might have made her strong, but also combative at times. You could see her cool kind of distance that Aquarius brings.

Her deep, sensual intensity can be seen in that Scorpio rising which added to her passionate nature.

She does have an inner planetary streak of Pisces. It is not just any Pisces streak. A magnetic and hypnotizing Venus in Pisces conjunct on again / off again Uranus in the fifth house. It creates a magnetic attractiveness, shows talent, creativity and romantic nature. It shows a love of jewelry and wealth. It is at a strong trine angle with an exalted Jupiter in Cancer, filled with graces in the 9th house, and it brought her many blessings. This leaves her with a grand trine in water signs. So on the inside, her energy had a special "diamond."

Perhaps the beauty of the deep violet eyes came from this water trine combined with the energy of the charming Moon in Libra, in the spiritual twelfth house. This also shows how she was someone who enjoyed others but needed some serious solitude to emotionally unwind.

Saturn in its own sign is strong for work ethics and in the third house placement made her strong willed.

"Big girls need big diamonds."

"I feel very adventurous. There are so many doors to be opened, and I'm not afraid to look behind them."

"The problem with people who have no vices is that generally you can be pretty sure they're going to have some pretty annoying virtues."

"I've always admitted that I'm ruled by my passions."

Pisces

March 15 TO APRIL 13

Ruled by Jupiter
Element of Water
Color: Yellow
Gemstone: Yellow Sapphire
Body: Feet

Piscean birthdays fall in the realm that tropical zodiac calls Aries. But when we apply Sidereal time we can see that there is a Pisces Sun behind these sensitive souls. If you thought you were an Aries…well you can go dream on. Embrace your gentle Piscean nature. This is one sun sign mix up that seems to be the most extreme. A tender spirited Pisces fitting into the action adventure suit of an Aries?

Everyone wants to be considered a spiritual Pisces. Jupiter and Water combine to bring wisdom and intuition. This is a compassionate, spiritual, and old soul sign. Who is the calm friend, that patient person, with the good advice? That's the Pisces person!

They can be very fined tuned and sensitive to a psychic degree. Ruled by Jupiter, they have an old soul quality that helps them be mellow reasoning souls. They have a deep capacity for knowing.

They can be artistic and sensitive. They are often married or in a relationship as they love affection. They are usually very patient with their partners and will want spend much time with them. They are not co-dependant but more inter-dependant.

They, as fishes, can lack structure and discipline so they may not excel with leadership and decision making.

This sign has experienced a full ride thru the zodiac, thru many lives. They have grown and evolved. It shows in their Pisces incarnation. Intuition defies logic here.

They just know things and help their friends be calm with their presence. Albert Einstein knew that a good imagination was an important part of being intelligent.

The planets of Jupiter and Venus are at their best in Pisces, showing their deeper understanding of the universe and of love.

Pisces Sun People:

Jerry Lewis - March 16
Edgar Caye - March 18
Bruce Willis - March 19
William Shatner - March 22
Joan Crawford - March 23
Reese Witherspoon - March 24
Aretha Franklin - March 25
Steve Tyler - March 26
Leonard Nimoy - March 26
Mariah Carey March 27
Quentin Tarantino - March 27
Fergie - March 27
Lady Gaga - March 28
Celine Dion - March 30
Vincent Van Gogh - March 30
Ewan McGregor - March 31
Johann Sebastian Bach - March 31
Marlon Brando - April 3
Eddie Murphy - April 3
Maya Angelou April 4
Heath Ledger - April 4
Robert Downey Jr - April 4
Pharell Williams - April 5
Billie Holliday - April 7
Jackie Chan - April7
Russel Crowe - April 7
Kristen Stewart - April 9
Steven Seagal April 10
Clare Danes April 12

PISCES Chart Study:

Maya Angelou
April 4, 1928
2:10PM
Saint Louis, MO
Rising Sign: Cancer
Sun Sign: Pisces

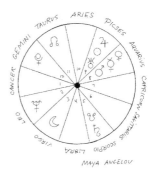

MAYA ANGELOU

It comes as no surprise that a beloved poet, memoirist and civil rights activist known for her wisdom has a Sun in Pisces, conjunct Jupiter, strong in its own sign, with a nearby radical Uranus, in the blessed 9th house. So she had a quite a golden gift of Jupiter.

Her book, I Know Why The Caged Bird Sings, made her the first African American woman to be on the non-fiction bestseller list. It was the late 1960s and she brought much to support a positive light of black women in American culture at the time.

She had a Cancer rising, which can create a very nurturing mother figure. She also had a moon in Virgo, which was mercury ruled, in the literary third house. So she and words were at one. She was thinking it, feeling it, and writing it as her therapy.

Her Mars, Mercury and Venus in Aquarius in the depths of the 8th house, showed a difficult early life, but it transformed her to become a force in adulthood. This stellium of planets was in social action and civil rights minded Aquarius. Also the traditional ruler of Aquarius, Saturn, in her 5th house, further reinforces her gift as a champion for the cause. She had also worked with Martin Luther King Jr as an organizer during the Civil rights Movement.

Her quotes and literary contributions and the way she shared her self shows her Piscean compassion for others and the wisdom it brings.

The 13 Zodiac Sign

Ophiuchus the Serpent Bearer: A Case for Sidereal Time

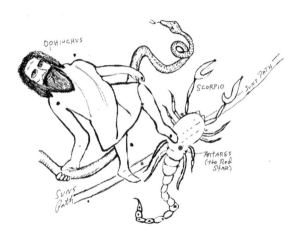

There was news of a recent "new sign" released. Its basically a sign next to Scorpio, that also shares the path of the sun. How it developed as a popular wave in astrology is as much a mystery as where tropical zodiac got started. Do we really need to add this extra sign? So I was looking for a logical reason. I think the ancients needed to split the sky in 12 to suit the rhythm of the Roman Calendar. It reflected the seasonal year brought on by the earths orbit. So I have feeling some committee or head astrologer somewhere in ancient times, decided upon Scorpio over Ophiuchus.

The astrological sky is logically split into twelve signs. The system of about 88 constellations maps the sky. In Astrology, we are concerning ourselves with the constellations that are behind the path of the sun. These constellations vary in size. When we consider 'signs' we talk the 30 degree arc, but constellations are not neatly just 30 degrees. It varies. Many astrologers happily adjust the signs to neatly conform to 30 degrees. Its called equal houses. Astrologers know when applying setting on their astrological software or app, that they can use the house systems that are even, or the ones that are astronomically accurate.

So its with this "13th" sign, it is said that Ophiuchus covers 17.75 degrees of the suns actual arc, while Scorpio only takes up 7° of arc. Yes, Ophiuchus toe is nearer to the suns path and stays in it longer than our Scorpion friend.

Many of the characteristics applied to Ophicius are similar to Scorpio descriptions. It also has similarities to a Nakshatra (27 star cluster system) from India. Ophiuchus correlates to the Nakshatra of Jyestha also shared by the later degrees of Scorpio, with similar qualities such as being passionate, jealous, intense and protective.

I am adding this chapter, not to go on about this new signs meanings, as much as how it supports the use of Sidereal time. Many people will need accurate and current astronomical information for this. So this 13th constellation can be used as a step toward Sidereal time and away from Tropical. A good astrologer will look at the sky or at least a planetarium app true star time to access Ophiuchus. This is a great experiment to I recommend to go to a planetarium app right now and check it out. So hopefully astrologers can accidentally discover Sidereal time because of Ophicius!

Thank you for taking your time to read this book.
But let's not waste time! Please do the planetarium app

experiment and see for yourself the truth of Sidereal time!
Hopefully we will get this knowledge about Sidereal time
to expand and gain ground in the mainstream.
It's time is here and we can help Western Astrology with this
24 degree adjustment back to where
True astronomy is aligned with Astrology.
I hope you will take from it some new
perspectives and action on astrology.

In light and love,
Trudy Sita

Printed in the United States
By Bookmasters